Self-Financing in Higher Education : Prospects and Retrospects

Self-Financing in Higher Education : Prospects and Retrospects

Dr. M.S. Singh
Principal
Digvijainath P.G. College
Gorakhpur (U.P.)

ADHYAYAN
Adhyayan Publishers & Distributors
New Delhi-110002

Published by
ADHYAYAN PUBLISHERS & DISTRIBUTORS
4378/4 B, 105, J.M.D. House, Murari Lal Street
Ansari Road, Darya Ganj, New Delhi-110002
Ph. : 011-23263018, 011-23277156, Fax : 011-23280028
E-mail : adhyayanpublishers@yahoo.com

Self-Financing in Higher Education : Prospects and Retrospects

Edition : 2010
ISBN : 978-81-8435-122-4

Printed in India

Published by Harish Chandra Yadav for Adhyayan Publishers & Distributors, Laser Typesetting at Net Graphics and Printed at Tarun Offset Printers, Delhi.

Editorial

The System of higher education in India at present is a big challenge; the challenge to face the rapid change of the 21st century with the effect of membership of W.T.O. along with our higher education system has been fully affected though the L.P.G.C., since 1991. The Liveralisation privatisation, globalisation and commercialisation are the four terms which are attracting the attention of educationists and policy makers in recent times. Therefore this seminar Self-Financing. Higher Education; Prospects and Retrospect" an attempt to discuss and deliberate on various phenomenon of self-financing higher education. It is rather impossible to look after each and every aspects of self-financing at higher education, therefore we select only six areas, such as- Genesis, Empowerment, Commercialisation, Relevance, Value, and Quality.

The main objective of this seminar into focus the Pron and Cons of self-financing system in higher education. It is the duty of scholars, thinkers and participants to look deep into the theme. I am confident; contribution and discussions whatever done by the delegates would be the guidelines for the regulatory authorities for higher education system.

So for this souvenir is concerned, it has been tried to make it more rich and attractive academically by incorporating the valuable articles received from the scholars of various universities. The main objective of the publication of this book to man ackledat and were about the detail matter whatever delevered by eminent educationists and door palimpsest.

I would like to seek the complete suggestions from all the knowledge reader.

—Dr. M.S. Singh
Editor and Convener

Preface

This project is an attempt to discuss and deliberate on various dimensions of self-financing in higher education. The need of education for preparing human beings for living is undeniable.The way of imparting education has been changing continuously. The socio-political and global initiatives have been impinging upon the quality and quantum aspects of education. Media and information technology have contributed no less to these aspects. The awareness towards need for educating the progeny has never been that intense as it is today. Consequently, the exponential demand for education in disciplines which have natural heritage and knowledge that has groomed abroad in new fields, resulted in multiplication of several branches of higher education. To need these challenges, the Government of India has made sincere efforts in pursuance of National Education Policy in education sector.

The recent phenomenon of self-financing educational institutions, have been facilitated by the several factors like, low access rate *i.e.* 7 percent. Indian system of higher education, in spite of being one the largest system of higher education of the world, uneven quality of education, rigidity of conventional university system and its unwillingness to innovate and change, intense need for education commensurate to world class standards due to globalization and shift in government's priority for education resulting in curtailed outlay for higher education.

There are different terminologies used in the context of globalization. Globalization is a term that has recently come into use along with LPGCM as such. The process of globalization in India had been initiated since 1980s. But it was speed up with the adoption of economic reform measures in 1991. After accepting the membership of WTO. The negotiations WTO on the "general agreement on trade in service" (GATE), about the liberalization of trade in education services revolve around such arguments. This has led to the entry of (for profit) entrepreneurs in the market of higher education. This acceptance gradually effecting the Indian Socio-cultural and educational area.

Self-financing/privatization means "Self-monitoring support for an enterprise." The focus of self-financing institutions is securing, provision, control and management of funds by a private agency. This is also known as self-supporting or self-sustaining private enterprise.

There are at least four versions of privatisation concepts, such as: (i) *The extreme version* of privatisation that implies total privatization, private college and universities being managed and funded by the private sector, *(ii)* The *strongform* of privatization where higher education is publicly provided but costs are fully recovered from the students, *(iii)* The *moderate form* of privatization where higher education is with a reasonable level of financed mobilized from non-governmental sources; and *(iv) The pseudo privatization* where higher education is privately provided at public expense.

The Present Debate

The debate of self-financing privatization of higher education is mainly revolving around two main issues, *viz., "Trading of Education"*and *"Role of Education"*. The protagonists of both the schools of though have strong arguments. Without having the clear understanding of both the perspectives, it is not possible to develop any rational policy framework. Let us first analyses both the arguments:

"Genesis of self-financing/privatization of higher education is not new phenomenon in

India and elsewhere. After the Second World War and in the Indian context from 1970s is the landmark of this concept. Its historical perspective is as old as education. Only aims of education are changing continuously according to the socio-cultural, political and economic change. Such as **'Siksha Dan Ki Vastu Hai'** now its reached to **'Siksha Ek Byavsai Hai'.** The total approach paper mainly divided into two parts such as under:

Trading of Education

The first and the foremost issue that has become a matter of hot debate and concern amongst all affected groups is 'trading of education.' The argument of protagonists of privatization is "The supply of education should be according to the individual and market needs. There should be free access of market players. The education is being treated as a product and the students as 'consumers'. There should be free competition in the market place. The market players should be able to select a product enter the market for profit. If the product is not in demand, they should be able to drop is or exit the market". Its means commercialization always concerned with the "Exploitation for the purpose of gaining profit."

The Role of Education

The counter argument to 'trading of education' is being linked with the larger stakes of the society in education. The issue of 'Role of Education' is being advanced.

The concept of the 'student as a consumer' and 'education as a product' fails to acknowledge the importance of higher education as a social tool and runs counter to the creation of knowledge based society, with democratic, tolerant and active citizens.

The concept of higher education as mere tradable product jeopardizes the academic freedom of universities, as markets fail and a self-out of education might lead to decreasing diversity and freedom of research in institutions of higher education.

Empowerment always concerned with the strengthen the natural as well as human resources. The for figure factual this reference, the Central/State Governments are going to empower of private sector only. Because the primary moto of government does not want to expend the money of those sector which are not in position to give the profit.

The main aim of value-based educations to make the students good citizens, who in true may share their responsibility in the changing set-up of the society in order to give the desired shape and image to the society, and the country at large. It is important to identify the values that are relevant to modern context, physical, social, economic, aesthetic, ethical and spiritual.

The conscience of higher education is shivering in the hand of policy-maker, parents administrators, managers and educational agencies such as (UGC, NCTE, NAAC., NIPA. & EDCIL) or other organization that control it. Keeping in mind the *Mushroom growth* in the number of higher educational institutes, it became imperative to assess their performance by some committees. The present scenario of self-financing scheme of higher education now being throttled and Ben playing in the hand of these supervisory agencies. There is exists uncertainty about NOC, affiliation, qualification, sub-standard selection of teacher, adhocism and allowing part time staff, ill paid persons to teach, the compromising attitude about norms and standards for establishment and development of institution of higher education. Along with in effective monitoring panel inspectors who became instrumental to satisfaction of these agencies. Therefore, deficiencies cannot be labeled as justified by any yardsticks. So these factors are barrier of relevance's value, and quality of higher education.

Above issues, whatever has been arised by me it is not last but least to look about. I am confident about contributions, and discussions whatever done by scholars. Therefore, it would be thought provoke and would result preparing guideline which the regulatory agencies/authorities would find help in redesigning the system of higher education in our country. It is daunting task before the state agencies, society and academic would be to sustain the quality, relevance, value, national needs, affordable fee structures and stop the commodification of education. This national seminar has been organized to sensitized them to various presenting issue and help them in evolving some effective solutions.

Contents

1

Self-Financing in Teacher Education and Issues Related with Quality Control

G.S. Bhattacharya

In this age of Liberalization, Privatization and Globalization (LPG), public money subsidy may become insufficient soon due to efforts to ensure access of education to all and ever increasing population in developing countries in general as India, in particular, economic resource development is an essential measure for proper development of human resources along with others like skillful teachers/ educators, effective communication system, classroom teaching-learning environment etc. The central government is aspiring to enhance educational budget more than double under Eleventh Five Years Plan but more stress is on school education. Higher and especially, the professional education like teacher education is not yet drawing more budget for opening new professional institutions to meet the growing demands and in such a situation, alternative may be the self-financing scheme on entry of private trusts, corporate houses, individuals, etc.

At the same time, it is well-apprehended that privatization of professional institutions may initiate the problem of commercialization aspiring corporate groups to consider education as a commodity and maximization of profit may become the target at the cost of quality. The issue related with quality control may raise other points concerned with morality, appropriate evaluation and training, development of teaching ability and competency, organisation of practicals and school-based experiences essential for pre-service teachers and so on. Quality control may require planning, management of the process of teacher education, feedback and reformation, financial budgeting and availability of instructional resources, manpower or human resource based planning, replanning the process, functioning of the system, evaluation of the system and remedial measures scheduling and application. If any self-financing teacher education institution is ready to use this quality control system/loop, the institution may progress well with possibilities of acquiring high status in terms of financial as well as production of quality teachers or production points.

2

Ensuring Education for High Status Group Through Commercialization

Joseph M. Wamutitu

In the present era of information communication technology, higher education is expected to reorient its activities and move from knowledge creation to one where knowledge is created in an inter-disciplinary way based upon the problems of the society that higher education is expected to solve. One of the goal of higher education is to help to reduce poverty by making education accessible to all. It is expected to address the basic essential goals of education: Learning to know, to do, to live together with others, and to be. This may form the foundation for lifelong learning in an effort to reduce poverty. However, by privatizing and commercializing higher education, we may deny most of the students to have an access to quality education especially in a country like India where majority of the youths are belonging to the low-middle income groups. Without quality higher education, the youth groups may not be able to reduce their size of families, improve family health, enhance economic prospects and social well being. Commercialization of higher education may lead to increase the chance of those who belong to the high socio-economic class to have an access for it. So, instead of reducing the poverty in the society, commercialization of higher education may lead the society towards economic disparity and ultimately cause socio-economic crisis.

3

A Study of Suffering and Dis-comfort among Teachers Working in Self-Financing Institutions of Higher Education

Dr. Rita Chauhan
Harish Kumar Singh

The World Bank report of 1994 highlights the, worth of higher education wherein it is considerable that institutions of higher learning benefit state and society in several ways:

They equip individuals with advanced knowledge and skills to discharge responsibility in government, business and professions, produce new knowledge research and at least serve as conduit for the transfer, adaptation and dissemination of knowledge generated elsewhere in the world. The taskforce constituted by World Bank and UNESCO during 2000 has also observed that higher education helps increase wages and productivity that directly enrich individuals and society.

According to the census 2001, the overall literacy rate in the country has gone up by 10 per cent during the last 10 years. The vision of *Serve Shiksha Abhyan* is to provide useful and relevant elementary education of satisfactory quality for all by 2010 and it is possible that more (8–10) of this freshly educated lots seek admission at college level in the next

8–10 years. As against the current capacity of eleven million college seats created in the last 150 years, we require to create an additional capacity of 8–11.7 million college seats in the coming 8–10 years. Obviously this is a gigantic task that cannot be addressed by the government alone.

Over the time, there has been emergence of new types of providers of higher education in India. Colleges started self-financing programs and grew rapidly. Today higher education is geared for the mass catering to meet the demand of a vibrant democracy committed to the principles of equity with the help of self-financing institutions. But there are several allegations on these type of institutions, *i.e.* financial exploitation of stakeholders, non-satisfactory library conditions, lack of resources, no security to teaching and non-teaching staff, bullying by management, lack of moral responsibility in teachers, low quality teaching etc.

Quality enhancement depends on teachers of the institutions. Therefore, the present study is directed to explore the suffering and discomfort among the teachers working in self-financing institutions.

Objectives

The present study was conducted with the main aim of assessing suffering and discomfort that exis among teachers working in self-financing institutions. The study also investigates the visible effects of suffering and discomfort among teachers on the quality of teaching-learning process.

Methodology

26 teachers were chosen from self-financing institutions of higher education by random sampling. It consists 13 male teachers and 13 female teachers.

Investigator negotiated with the teachers.

Findings

Following facts were concluded by the investigator after the negotiation:

1. Extra amount is charged from the students apart from their notified fee.
2. Teachers are not appointed according the norms of

UGC. Teacher-student ratio is very poor. Teachers are not able to give individual attention to their students.

3. In some self-financing institutions teachers are not paid their according to government norms. In some institutions only part time teachers are appointed with very low salary.
4. Due to low payment skilled and qualified teachers are not attracted for self-financing institutions. Hence, stakeholders do not get qualified and skilled teachers.
5. In many self-financing institutions NET qualified or Ph.D. holder teachers are not getting proper salary in proper way. So, they do not feel themselves morally responsible or accountable for teaching-learning process.
6. Due to low payment and uncomfortable working conditions teachers feel themselves underemployed.
7. Teachers do not take interest in participating in good practices for quality enhancement.
8. Teachers are busy in searching regular job opportunities, they have no time for their professional development.
9. In search of secured appointment teachers are moving towards other areas, they are loosing their interest in this noble profession. Many teachers who are NET qualified or Ph.D. holders have applied for the post of Asstt. Registrar in University of Allahabad.
10. In these situations teachers suffer with anxiety, stress and insecurity, they fail to pay attention towards the enrichment of teaching contents and teaching techniques.
11. Such teachers always take teaching as a job not as a mission. They do not try to their develop their skills to interact with their students.
12 These teachers always believe that their duty is only delivering lecture in classroom. They do not believe in innovations.
13. In some institutions teachers are appointed only for 8–10 months. They feel insecure whether they will

be called in the next session or not.

14. Teachers get only fix payment and there is no arrangement of pension, fund, etc. Hence, there is anxiety in them as to how they will carry in future.
15. Teachers working in self-financing institutions do not get due respect in society. Due to their non-permanent nature of job there is occurrence of many kinds of sufferings related with self-respect, stratification, future prospects, social standing etc.
16. Some institutions have both types of courses self-financing as well as aided, teachers under aided scheme get appointment and salary from the government according to the norms in respectful manner, while teachers working under self-financing scheme face humiliation.
17. The teachers under the pressure of the Management Committee as well as the Administration. In order to keep their job secured the teachers have to keep the Management and Administration happy. Teachers have to perform unwanted work also.
18. The institutions having both regular and self-financing teachers, self-financing teachers have to face a second hand treatment by regular teachers.

Effects

1. Reduced rate of working efficiency.
2. Reduced of quality and quality control of teaching-learning process.
3. Low moral among teaching members.
4. Generation of tensed atmosphere in the campus.
5. High rate of absenteeism.
6. Reduced rate of excellence in teaching-learning process.
7. Depression and stress among teachers.
8. Increased rate of violence.
9. Opens door to legal side.
10. Lack of quality management.
11. Lack of student participation in best practice.
12. Weak emotional bond with the institutional bond with their institutions.

13. Scope for developing negative perception of the institution by the teachers.

Suggestions

The higher education sector in India is considered to be the second largest system in the world. The national goals of establishing higher education institutions are directed towards creating human resource assets capable of generating national wealth and serving as instruments of social change. Molding the attitudes and competence of the students during their formative years becomes the key responsibility of academic institutions. Students coming from high quality institutions become performing assets in the progress of the nation. If teachers are not comfortable, not getting job satisfaction, working under various pressure, no institution can fulfill nation's ambition of creating capable human resource assets.

Investigator feels that Government should take care of this matter. The University, from which the institution is attached, should be vigilant that teachers appointed are qualified and paid salary according to norms. There should be very synergetic relationship among teachers and members of management committee. Time-to-time meetings should be organized for the catharsis, as catharsis is a very good technical instrument for removing stress, tensions and other psychological problems. In self-financing institution working conditions of teachers should be improved. It is the duty of State, Society and Parent Institution to keep control on the management committee and administrative machinery of the self financing institutions.

References

1. *University News*, Association of Indian University, Vol. 45, No. 02.
2. The Economist, 1997, A Survey of Higher Education.
3. MHRD, (2006), Annual Report, Ministry of Human Resource.
4. Jayram, N. (2000), The fall of the Guru, the Decline of the Academic Profession.

4

Quantitative Growth and Quality Control in Higher Education: Role of IQAC

Dr. Kajal Deb

Quality control is a by-product of ongoing efforts to define the objectives of an institution, to have a work plan to achieve them and to specify the checks and balances to evaluate the degree to which each of the tasks is fulfilled. Hence devotion and commitment to improve rather than mere institutional control is the basis for assuring quality. Quality is an abstract word unless related to definable and measurable characteristics of the products involved.

"There is a moving debate about quality and excellence in higher education. Quality is inclusive; it is the benchmark that every institution must achieve. Excellence is exclusive (Mukhopadhyaya, 2006)." Quality control refers to the process of verifying whether everything occurs in conformity with the plan adopted, the instructions issued and principles established. It is expected to identify weakness and errors with the intension of rectifying them and preventing recurrence.

The quantity of a product is negatively correlated with its quality. When quantity of production is increased without corresponding increase or improvement in the input, the quality of the product is bound to deteriorate. This is exactly what has happened with our education system. The huge quantitative expansion has taken place at the cost of quality, especially during the post-independence period. During the period of six decades since 1947, there has been a phenomenal quantitative growth of higher education system. The number of universities and colleges have gone up from only 20 in 1947 to over 361 at present (2006-07). The number of affiliated colleges has gone up from 500 to 16,000 during the same period. The total enrolment of students has also witnessed corresponding increase from less than 2 lakhs to over 77 lakhs (Gautam, 1999). Quantitatively, there has been a remarkable development characterized by many fold increase in the number of universities and colleges along with student enrolment. This has caused serious problems in maintaining classroom discipline and has led to deterioration in the quality of teaching and research. It has been seen that about 45 percent of the affiliated colleges are listed in the category of non-viable college and are not eligible for UGC grant, because, these colleges do not fulfill the minimum requirements for its purpose. Consequently, there are full registers but empty classrooms.

With phenomenal expansion during the post-independence period, the higher education system in India has become one of the largest in the world. As stated by Naik (1982) the post-independence period may be described literally as the 'Era of Higher education' in Indian educational history. Since this quantitative growth was in an unplanned manner, Education Commission (1964-66) expressed a grave concern over the deteriorating quality of higher education. The Commission made many important recommendations in this context, which included selective admission pattern in colleges and university and establishment of major universities and autonomous colleges. The National Policy on Education (1986) also made some important proposals for the quantitative and qualitative development of higher education in India. The University Grants Commission (UGC) had been given the responsibility of determining and maintaining standard of higher education and disbursement of grants to eligible universities and colleges according to requirements.

The system of higher education in India has grown so large that the entire financial input available is used up in keeping the system going, rather than, initiating new schemes. Even though the financial inputs in higher education have increased almost ten times during the last 50 years, there is always a resource crunch. The cost of higher education has gone up so high that the funding agency like UGC cannot afford to finance all the institutions indiscriminately irrespective of their quality. Therefore, assessment of performance of higher education institutions and grading them according to quality stands essential . The NPE, 1986 and POA, 1992, also stated that "excellence of higher education institutions is a function of many aspect, self-evaluation and self- improvement are important if a mechanism is set-up, which will encourage self-assessment in institutions and also assessment and accreditation by a council The quality, process, participation, achievement, etc. will be constantly monitored and improved."

In pursuance of above recommendations, the UGC constituted a committee to finalize rules and regulations and finally in 1994, the National Assessment and Accreditation Council (NAAC) came into existence. The NAAC had been given the responsibility of assessing and accrediting institutions of higher education. After considerable research and experimentation, NAAC has standardized a comprehensive model to measure the, quality and releyance of the educational process in colleges and universities.

Role of NAAC

NAAC has been established with a vision to make quality the defining element of higher education in India through a combination of self and external quality evaluation, promotion and sustenance initiatives. The NAAC strives to work for quality enhancement in higher education with the following mission:

- To arrange for periodic assessment and accreditation of institutions of higher education.
- To stimulate the academic environment for promotion of quality of teaching-learning and research in higher education institutions.

- To encourage self-evaluation accountability autonomy and innovations in higher education.
- To undertake quality-related research studies, consultancy and training programs.
- To collaborate with other stakeholders of higher education for quality enhancement.

UGC has decided to make accreditation mandatory for institutions to receive their funds. The accreditation is being done on seven parameters:

(i) Curricular aspects.
(ii) Teaching, learning, evaluation.
(iii) Research consultancy and extension.
(iv) Infrastructure and learning resources.
(v) Student support and progression.
(vi) Organization and management.
(vii) Healthy practices.

Role of Internal Quality Assurance Cell IQAC

In pursuance of the National Action Plan of the NAAC for performance, evaluation, assessment and accreditation and quality upgradation of institutions of higher education the NAAC has proposed that every accredited institution to establish an IQAC as a post -accreditation quality sustenance measure. Since quality enhancement is a continuous process, the IQAC is supposed to work towards realizing the goals of quality enhancement and sustenance.

The basic purposes of the IQAC are:

(i) To develop a system for conscious consistent and catalytic action to improve the academic and administrative performance of the institution.
(ii) To assure all the stakeholders connected with higher education about the quality of education provided by the institutions.

Realizing the above objectives the following functions are expected from the IQAC:

(i) To act as a nodal agency of the institution for quality related activities.
(ii) Documentation of various activities leading to quality improvement.

(*iii*) Organization of workshops, seminars on quality related themes.

(*iv*) Development and application of quality benchmarks/ parameters for the various academic and administrative activities of the institution.

(*v*) Preparation of the Annual Quality Assurance Report (AQAR) to be submitted to NAAC based on the quality parameters. This report consist of Plan of Action chalked out by IQAC in the beginning of the session and outcome achieved along with a detailed Plan of Action for the next session. It also consist of informations in 41 areas related to teaching, learning, evaluation, research and institutional infrastructures and other activities.

The composition of IQAC depends on the size and complexity of the institution. It includes the head of the institution, a few senior administrative officers, a number of teachers and members from management one/two nominees from local society and a teacher as the coordinator of IQAC. It is necessary for the members of the IQAC to shoulder the responsibilities of generating and promoting awareness in the institution and to devote time for working out the procedural details. This will help the colleges in planning and monitoring.

The role of the coordinator of IQAC is crucial in ensuring the effective functioning of all the members and implementing the functions. The operational features and functions expected of the IQAC are broad-based to facilitate institutions towards academic excellence and institutions may adopt them to their specific needs.

The IQAC has to ensure that whatever is done in the institution for 'education' is done efficiently and effectively with high standards. To achieve this the IQAC has been given following responsibilities:

- To get the Students Questionnaire (provided by NAAC) filled by the students. It consist of the feedback given by the students regarding assessment of teachers and their qualities of teaching.
- To maintain a self- assessment record of the teachers,

which they are supposed to fill regularly.

- To encourage innovations and initiatives in the field of teaching, learning and evaluation.
- To motivate students participation in classroom teaching.
- To ensure regular assessment of students achievement by the teachers.

As far as the vision, objectives, functions and responsibilities of the IQAC is concerned, it is bound to enhance the quality culture in the institutions of higher education and promote the academic atmosphere at large. But, there are various constraints which the IQAC has to face in putting its functions into practice. Some of them are as follows:

- Lack of infrastructure.
- Lack of support from other stakeholders of higher education.
- Lack of interest/ motivation to work towards quality enhancement.
- Lack of proper, working atmosphere in the institution.

The IQAC has to face many difficulties in shouldering its responsibilities:

- The questionnaire provided by NAAC is quite difficult for the students to understand. Their answers are prejudiced and sometimes they are scared to answer genuinely. All this makes the practice of filling the questionnaire unfruitful.
- Maintaining self-assessment record by the teachers is again not easy and sometimes not reliable also.
- Innovations and initiatives can only be taken if there is some inner motivation to do the same, it cannot be forced externally:
- Students participation cannot be ensured unless there is proper support and interest from their side.

Suggestions

Following are some suggestions which can be incorporated to overcome the difficulties faced by the IQAC:

- Teachers assessment on the basis of students'

response given in the questionnaire should be discouraged because, firstly, it is not reliable and secondly, the students' answers are biased.

- Feedback may be taken from the students about teachers quality of teaching and other activities by providing them a short and simple questionnaire or it may be done on-line.
- Grading of teachers according to students' response should be discouraged.
- Self-evaluation of teachers as well as non-teaching staff may be encouraged.
- Students, participation should be encouraged in classroom activities but not in evaluation process.
- The members of IQAC should establish good rapport with themselves and with the teachers as well to discuss initiatives to be taken to ensure quality enhancement.

Inspite of the mushroom growth of higher educational institutions there is large scale discontentment among the university graduates. There is a need of some drastic change in the total quality management in higher education. Quality should be accepted as an attitude of the mind because positive attitude towards one's work play a more critical role in quality control and enhancement. Now, we should shift emphasis from linear expansion to qualitative development of higher education.

In todays changing scenario of society, India needs to look into the quality of higher education, its declining status and must work together to enhance its quality, which needs to be nurtured and protected in a continuous manner.

"Quality is a journey not a destination."

References

1. Chauhan, C.P.S., *Modem Indian Education Policies, Progress and Problems,* Kanishka Publishers and Distributors, New Delhi, 2004.
2. Gautam, H., *Infancy to Excellence, Developmental Stages of Educational Institutions,* University News, AIU, New Delhi, 1991.
3. Mukhopadhyaya, M.M., Keynote Address in the

inaugural session of the National Seminar on, *Developing Quality Culture in Higher Education.: Innovations and Initiatives,* Allahabad, November 18-9, 2006.

4. Naik, J.P., Education Commission and after Allied Publishers Private Limited, New Delhi, 1971.
5. *National Policy on Education (NPE), 1986 and A Programme of Action (POA),* New Delhi, 1986 and 1992.
6. www.naac-india.com

5

Privatization of Higher Education *vs* Commercialization

Dr. Sarita Rani
Sunil Kumar

Prior to independence, the growth of institutions of higher education in India was very low. After independence, the number of institutions has increased significantly. Before independence, there were only three universities and increased there are 384 universities open universities, agricultural universities, women universities, language universities and medical universities. In addition, there are also thousands of colleges. 74.18 lakh students take admission in these colleges but being the increase in population its ratio is quite less. Many students are still unable to attain higher education. If we wish to arrange higher education for all eligible and desirous candidates, we need to establish much more colleges and for which government has to expend a lot of money.

Higher education in India is in deep financial strain with escalating costs and increasing needs on the one hand and shrinking budgetary resources on the other. The only alternative many be the privatization of higher education for fulfilling the increasing needs and demands and for providing qualitative education. But as far as qualitative improvement in education we see that current education system is preparing a large number of educated unemployed candidates. We see three or four lakhs unemployed register their name in employment offices. Apart from this a number of educated unemployed are there who do not make registration in the employment offices. These students are mentally frustrated and misguided and indulge in various illegal works.

Investment in Higher Education

If we look at the investment made by government on the higher education it is clear that government is focusing its attention on primary education not on her education. The share of higher education in total planned resources increased for 0-71% the First Five Year Plan to 1.24 %.

During this period 'World Bank also presented its report on investment in education in developing countries in which it suggested the investment by parents on higher education. In the year 1991, Narsimha Rao Government followed the suggestion of World Bank. At the same time UGC has made 35% cut in the higher education and instructed all the universities and institutions of higher education should make efforts to raise their own resources.

In 1993, Punnayya Samiti presented its report to UGC and gave suggestion for privatization of higher education and suggested institutions to raise their resources by raising fee levels and encouraging private donations.

World Bank report also suggested that a great proportion of investment should be made on primary education for that to remove illiteracy and poverty from the country.

Mahmoodar Rahman Committee and Anand Krishnan Committee also presented their reports and recommended privatization of education as institutions of higher education should make efforts to raise their own resources.

Ambani-Birla Report on Privatization of Higher Education

On 24th April, 2001 'A policy frame work for remarks in Education' was presented by Mukesh Ambani and Kumar Manglam. This report was prepared with keeping in mind the educational needs of India up to 2015. In this report it is noted that in 2015 the population of India will be 125 crores in which 45 crores persons will be between 5 to 24 year of age and 34 crores will be 5 years of age group and for them there must be compulsory education for class 1–12 and 20% of the rest of the 11 crores *i.e.* 2.2 crores persons will be in position to get higher education and for higher education twenty-seven thousand four hundred seventy-one colleges and universities have to be opened where as primary and secondary level 07 lakhs 31 thousand 667 primary schools and 23,556 secondary schools have to be established.

According to this report near about forty-two thousand crore rupees will be needed for higher education up to 2015 and apart from this government has to spend Rs. 11,000 crore for construction of new institutions.

With declining or stagnant budgets government is unable to spend such a lot of money. Therefore money investment in ratio of 40 to 60 in private and government is recommended. Definitely higher education will be very costly and only rich class will be able to attain higher education.

Some other impractical recommendation are also presented in this report. Student loan program has been the most prominent methods that is currently suggested as an effective solution to the problem of financing higher educations. Many nationalized banks in India have begun to offer a variety of loan to students for higher education within the country and abroad but parents are not willing to take this loan as they are feared about their payment as they are not sure about the job after getting higher education.

Besides this the report also recommended to make the curriculum vocation and to take national level test SET, GRE and GIMAT for admission. Refresher courses for teachers to promote further researches and to make institutions to become financially self-reliant. In this way the report has recommended for privatization of higher education.

In the very recent period growth of private colleges especially Engineering and medical colleges has been remarkable. Private universities also recommended on 29th June, 2001. U.P. Government has decided to open two universities first is Viklang Kalyan University in Chitrakoot and other is information technology. University by Maharshi Yogi Foundation.

Suggestions for Impressive Privatization

The rapid growth of self-financing private colleges is a recent phenomenon. There are a large number of private colleges in the general and technical education spheres. These private colleges do provide financial relief to the government in providing higher education but at huge and long-term economic and nor-economic cost of the society. They are result of private enterprises and initiatives. These private colleges charge donations and capitation fees. The government wants to encourage private initiatives in higher education but not commercialization. The issue of concern with regards to the privatization of education is, what should be the role of the state. There are many academicians who favour privatization of education with a clause in the form of same role of the state. The role of the state may be in the following form:

- *(a)* To see that the basic norms such as qualified personnel are put in far imparting the educational services.
- *(b)* The basic infrastructure is available with the private institutions to curb the wider disparities in terms of access to education.
- *(c)* To see that the standard and efficiency is maintained by private institutions.
- *(d)* To bring the concept of equity in light for deserving students of law income group.

These are some of the major functions that state is expected to perform while going for privatization of education like Government should allow only reputed institutions so that they may not commercialize. There should be fee concession for low income and meritorious students. One-third seals should be reserved for poor and meritorious students. The admission in these institutes should be on merit basis and for which a strict rule arid policy should be made and followed.

For the selection of qualified and learned teachers a commission should be organized.

In the management committee of these colleges there

should be representatives of educationists, teachers, investors and social service organization. There should be proper and regular checking of the teaching system of these colleges. There should be correct ratio of teacher and student.

These suggested reforms needs to be carried gradually in different phases.

Government should also check that there should be proper classrooms, laboratories and libraries in these colleges.

Many personal managements are trying to open self-financing colleges. But there are some irregularities found in these colleges as after they provide a minimum salary to their teachers and appoint unexperienced unqualified teachers. They charge too much fees and these are the limitations of these institutions. The growth of private initiatives has also increased the concern for quality to increase access to education, India has encouraged private initiatives. The government run colleges are few and privately managed trusts or societies have founded the greater number of colleges about 70 percent of the total. Most of the private colleges established before 1980s get more than 95 percent of their finance support from the state government and they are called grant in aid colleges. With limited resources government could not extent financial support to the private initiatives established after the 1980s. These colleges run on student fees. Though self-financing they have to comply with the rules of government and affiliating university. The direct public expenditure of public funded institution, the high fee structure of self-financing colleges and substandard facilities available in some of these institutions have raised the question of value for money and hence the need for an effective mechanism for quality assurance. NCTE, NETRI and UGC and Directorate of Education should check the administration and examination system of these self-financing colleges.

6

Privatization of Higher Education in India : Problem and Prospects

Dr. Dinesh Kumar
Dr. Sandeep Kr. Agrawal
Krishna Murari Mishra

The private initiative in education, especially higher education is not altogether new to India. Some of the leading universities namely, the Banaras Hindu University and the Aligarh Muslim University came up with the efforts of certain dedicated individuals and financial support of the community at large. Again, a large number of educational institutions in the country especially those concerned with general and professional higher education have been established on private and voluntary initiative with or without financial subsidy from the government. In the context of the current changing social and economic fabric of the country, it appears almost certain to go in for private funding of education. The recent paradigm shift in Indian economic and political philosophy has led to the demand of private universities so as to meet the challenge of contemplated open economy and the demand for qualitative human resources and high level of R&D. There are views for and against privatization of higher education in India. While some have started criticizing the concept even before it has come to be defined and taken off the ground, others consider it very useful and indeed inevitable. So much so that proposals for setting up private universities affiliating the privately funded institutions are being discussed. For one thing, there is no denying the fact that higher education is comparatively less expensive in India even though under-developed countries like Bangladesh and developed ones like the US, Japan, Australia and many others have successfully switched over to privatization of education without making it a crass. Can India also think on these lines especially if the money earned can be 'ploughed back' into the educational sector for its own improvement? A clear cut policy of the Government of India regarding privatization of higher education is unfortunately not available at the present moment. We wonder if there is one at all. At any rate, the move is lacking in transparency. One thing is, however, clear from the occasional official pronouncements that there is a need for supplementing Government measures by the efforts of the non-government organizations and the institutions themselves to generate resources.

Private Station of Higher Education in the USA and UK

In the United States of America the concept of private universities is an integrated part of the political and economic philosophy of consumer sovereignty. The state intervention in education is exerted indirectly by regulating consumer response. In keeping with this view of philosophy, the state regulates its concerns about access and equity by providing funds to institutions of higher learning or establishing institutions under its control. The state also largely finances students directly by paying for their education as consumers. If one has inadequate means to pay for education, the state would, provide resources for the same. The socalled 'voucher system' and various schemes of scholarships and loans come in this category. Thus, the state indirectly subsidises education either through educational institutions or through the receiver of education. Along side state funding, American education is the responsibility of the local governments, parents, students, alumni and, most importantly, private and voluntary bodies. There are universities which are purely private with no governmental subsidy whatsoever. The universities of Yale, Princeton, Perdue amongst others are the world famous universities known for high quality education available to those who could afford to pay.

Thus, there is a dual system of public and private education with traditional distinctions based primarily on the means of their financing and the nature of control. The United States is committed to preserving this dual system of higher education by maintaining both public as well as private institutions.

The higher education system in the UK shares some of its features with those in the USA. Self-governing nature of the universities and their administrative and financial autonomy are most important. The Universities of Oxford and Cambridge which are nearly 800 years old and the Universities of London and Durham founded in the early part of the 19th century, though not strictly private in the American style and manner, are independent and self-governing academic bodies. Their funds, except those required for the capital projects come from their own resources such as income from endowments, consultancy income of the faculty, donations, support from industry, voluntary subscriptions from alumni and tuition fees.

Financial Problem in Higher Education: Suggestions

Lack of adequate funds in education is the most crucial issue. While overall investment in education as a proportion of the Gross Domestic Product (GDP) has gone up from 1.2 percent in 1950s to 3.7 percent in the 1990s, it is still below the norm of 6 percent as stated in the National Policy on Education. University education has particularly been hit hard. Most higher education institutions all over the country are facing acute financial crisis. Two important questions immediately intervene themselves: One, what is the justification for so radically changing the 40-year old policy of state support to higher education, and two, how could the state extend financial support to higher education at a time when the country is facing severe resource crunch? Since provision of free and compulsory education at the elementary stage is a constitutional commitment, budgetary allocation for this sector of education is continuously on increase while the university and higher education has got a raw deal for the sixth year in succession. This is in keeping with the declared objective of the Union Government that the lion's share of funding for higher education must come from sources other than the government. The consequence of inadequate investment in higher education is serious. While the universities are at pain in persuading the government for increased budgetary allocations, some of them have simultaneously taken measures for generating funds of their own.

It is high time the university system resorted to long-term resource planning instead of taking the state support for granted. Each university will now have to identify avenues of resource generation, both internal as well as external, depending upon the nature of its program offerings and the locale. The Punnayya Committee set-up by the UGC and the Swamina than Panel of the AICTE have made some broad recommendations in this regard. The internal measures, amongst other things, may include proper utilization of funds, general economy in expenditures, pooling and sharing of departmental and institutional resources and most importantly, rationalisation of fee structure. As far the external resources, the important avenues include donations from alumni, philonthropists and others, consultancy, university-industry interaction, etc. In most institutions of higher education, at present, the tuition fees contribute very little towards earnings while the recurring expenditure on each student is much higher. In fact, an upward revision of fees is over due. The need to raise the tuition fees to at least 20 percent of the recurring expenditure per student generally and at a still higher level in higher professional and technical courses is being advocated. Increase in fees from the foreign students at further higher levels is being talked about by reserving seats for them in select institutions like the LIT and the IIMS. While measures such as these appear realistic, their repercussions need to be thoroughly assessed before taking some definite decision in the matter. Particularly, interests of poor students generally and those Indian students who are pitted against the foreign students admitted on the basis of higher fees need to be protected.

By far the least controversial avenue of generating additional resource is that of tapping the philonthropists, alumni and others such as business houses and industrial concerns for voluntary contributions. In order to encourage this the Government of India's financial act provides for 100 percent tax exemption in respect of donations by a tax payer to a university or institution of national eminence. Again, University-industry interaction is becoming a plank in this direction. The Swaminathan panel has suggested building up a reservoir of funds by collecting educational cess from industries and other user organizations. Setting up of an Educational Development Bank of India initially with shares of Rs. 1000 crore each by the State Governments, Central Government and international financial agencies has also been suggested. Raising money through consultancy work or job assignment by institutions to industries or other professional organizations is yet another avenue being profusely recommended. As an incentive, part of this money goes to individual scholars while the rest is added to the funds of the university. It is pertinent to mention here the official view that avenues generated through enhanced fee structure, consultancy and other activities would not be offset against government grants with the industries consideration 'adoption' of one or more institutions of higher education.

To sum up we can say that the Government of India in its National Education Policy, 1986, and thereafter World Bank report on higher education in developing countries, the liberalization since 1991 by the Narsimha Rao Government at the centre and after that the Punnaia Committee report in 1992, Mehmoodar Rahaman Committee, Anand Krisnan Committee report, Ambani-Birla report in 2000, it is quite clear that government is not going to bear the expense/subsidy provided to higher education by 2015. It is estimated that by 2015 the population of India will be approx. 125 crores and to bear the higher education expense Rs. 42,000 crore is needed p.a. therefore it is suggested in Ambani-Birla report to open private universities and for this an act must be passed by Parliament. The report also suggested that to meet such private higher education a system of scholarship and educational loan must be started in the country.

As we all known, providing increased access to education, meeting the challenge of equity and improving the quality of education all entail large investment. It is all the more necessary to ensure continuous inflow of funds needed for implementing and carrying out relevant program and activities. But then there does exist the problem of resource crunch. A suggested way out is exploring additional avenues of generating systems own resources instead of being fully dependent on the state exchequer. It is imperative here that the higher education system has to seek participation both of the government as well as private and voluntary bodies. Some amount of private funding thus appears inevitable for making up the deficit caused by inadequate state funding. In the last, we are can say that in privatization of higher education the following crucial questions must be kept in mind by the government:

1. What is the rationale for privatizing higher education?
2. What exactly are the issues related to access and equity in higher education and how would privatization tackle them?
3. Will private effort be able to generate the requisite finance for higher education?
4. How has privatization delivered goods in the educational systems abroad?
5. Will private funding of the university system eventually be a substitute to the statutory and constitutional requirement of the state to maintain institutions of higher learning?
6. Will private funding be really available for courses other than those concerned with professional and technical higher education?
7. Will privatization not lead to commercialization?
8. Is commercialization of higher education in national interest?
9. Will privatization not adversely affect interests of the poor and other backward sections of the society?

7

Privatization of Education *vs.* Commercialization

Mr. Syed Hasan Qasim

In India, over the years, there have been private initiatives in education initially for philanthropic reasons and eventually in professional and even in general higher education not only to meet the growing demands but also to realize the huge and quick profits potential. Privatization of higher education has emerged in several forms and types in the recent decade in India. One, privatization within government higher education institutions take place in the form of introducing self-financing courses within government institutions; two, converting government-aided private institutions into private self-financing institutions; three, allowing to expand self-financing private institutions with recognition and also without recognition, which may be termed as commercial private higher education institutions. Commercial private higher education emerges from market forces and tied to economic and global forces. They thrive on the principles of commercialism, primarily focus on vocational courses and highly pragmatic. Their commercial thrust is training jobs, indeed, part of the curriculum is industrial training. Not only training for jobs but also place their students in well-paid jobs. This indeed speaks about the strong industry—institution linkages. They are narrowly focused, rather micro-specific in designing their course and training. This narrow focus is their strength as well weakness. It is a strength as long as there is demand for such specific nature of the courses and a weakness once such a demand is satiated. Moreover, the built-in set-up / infrastructure do not allow them to diversify. They cater to the unmet demands or rather demand absorbing from the non-university higher education sector.

Ownership of these private institutions ranges between a spectrum of substantially weaker and stronger commercial institutions. Indeed, there are chain of institutions from Kinder garden to higher levels of education by well-known business groups and corporate sector. Since 1993 with the Supreme Court judgment, growth of commercial higher education in the name of capitation fee or self-financing colleges is mushrooming. The private institutions include colleges, training centers, etc. Neither the Department of Education nor the University Grants Commission collect, compile and publish the information on the size and growth of institutions and enrolments on this rapidly growing private higher education.

There are also different types of these private institutions—Many of the self-financing engineering colleges and management institutions are affiliated to the conventional universities (examples as found in Tamil Nadu, Karnataka and Andhra Pradesh). In which, the course structure, design, curriculum, and the pattern of examination fall within the purview of the national or state pattern. On the other side, several of these self-financing private institutions are also non-affiliating to any universities and cater to the demands of the corporate sector nationally and internationally. Whether the private institutions follow multi-faculty or discipline are decided by the individual institutions. Since the programs and courses are market-driven and each private institution decides on their own the course and subjects it offers. Hence, they also have a free hand to introduce new programs and discard the old.

Student is the power while faculty is weak in these private institutions. Indeed, the faculty lack the position, power and autonomy as they traditionally enjoy at universities. Basically they serve to students and their practical orientations in commercial private institutions. These institutions rely on part-time faculty and may be drawn from full-time faculty at public universities (and hence do not add to further employment opportunities). When employing full-time faculty, they pay meager salary. Perhaps many of them have neither practical nor academic expertise and lack training.

The finances of these private enterprises seem to be free to raise and deploy resources to meet their own norms. Private universities elsewhere, for instance in USA mobilize the resources of about 30 to 40 percent of the recurring cost of education from students. Remaining 60–70 of the recurring cost are generated from endowments, alumni and other sources (Ziderman and Albatch, 1995). On the contrary, fee in these private enterprises in India are exhorbitant as they fully depend upon student payments. Indeed, these institutions make huge profits, sometimes recover more than their recurring costs (full of recurring cost plus part of the capital cost). Such institutions survive as long as there is a demand for their services and the students are willing to pay for such job directed training.

The Government of India in its Prime Minister's Council on Trade and Industry, appointed a committee to suggest required reforms in the education sector, along with other sectors (headed by M. Ambani and K. Birla). It strongly suggested for full cost recovery (user pays principle) from students even in public higher education institutions through hike in fees and introduction of self-financing courses and seats; shifting of resources from higher to primary level of education that government should leave higher education altogether to the private sector and confine itself to elementary and secondary education. Further, the report urged the private university bill to be passed and also suggested that the user-pays principle be strictly enforced in higher education, supplemented by loans and grants to economically and socially backward sections of society (Ambani-Birla, 2001). In addition, number of foreign universities and franchise of multinational educational (business) centers compete in developing their own centers in India at a full cost recovery basis.

It is important to note that in the US, drive for efficiency and profits are categorically powerful among the private higher education providers. In developing countries like India, it is only the profit, which thrives these institutions and efficiency is jeopardized. Further, the important dimensions of complementarily and competition found in the US private higher education sector boosts the growth and survival of both the public and private higher institutions, which is conspicuously absent in India.

There are a number of important factors that led to emergence and rapid expansion of private higher education in India. They are classified here as the conventional pull and push factors. In addition to these, the external factors that have been conducive for the growth of private higher education is also discussed.

Pull Factors

All over the world including India, there has been rapid expansion and demand for higher education known as massification of higher education. The conventional university sector is not able to cater to the demands of the new sections of the rapidly growing eligible age group population for higher education. As an alternative, private enterprises are sought to accommodate this evolving pressure on higher education in various forms, types and levels.

Conventional university courses are not able to cater to the immediate demands of the market as it takes considerable amount of time for a change within the formal higher education/university system. This academic inflexibility boosted the rapid development of private initiatives in higher education. Perhaps, many providers/stakeholders in many of these private institutions are the one who struggled to change the formal system to suit to the needs of the students who, in turn, demand depending upon the marketability of a course, the emphasis being pragmatism.

The conventional institutions lack the responsiveness of higher education to labor market demands implying business participation in governing boards of institutions, the creation of financial incentives for joint industry-university research, corporate-sponsored internships for students, and part-time academic appointments for professionals from the productive sector. Alternatively, such a nexus between academics and industry is met by private institutions with multi-disciplinary and/or inter-disciplinary courses, which are short-term in nature with a very narrow focus. Hence, led to proliferation of short-term/market-oriented courses. However, leaving a few reputed private higher learning institutions, majority of them are education shops catering to the majority of the students, who are willing to pay with a desperate hope to get into the job market.

In short, these private institutions marketed their service in technology courses varying from hi-tech to fashion technology; management courses ranging from institutional management to hotel management; and promised to produce not only employable youth but also to place them in jobs.

Push Factors

Expenditure compression referred as resource constraint of the government on account of economic reforms led to financial privatization of higher education in various forms such as reduced allocation to higher education (decline in public expenditures and plan allocation on higher education see Table 1 and Chart 3); introduction of cost-recovery measures within public institutions and directed policy measures toward privatization of higher education. Government of India introduced the Private Universities Establishment and Regulation Bill in 1995. The bill is still pending in the Parliament because the private sector was not interested in several clauses in the bill — primarily on the clause on the provision of scholarship for the economically and socially backward sections of the population. Though, there have been deliberations on the private sector initiatives in higher education in different forums, there is no clear perspective on the issue. Yet another important factor is the deteriorating quality of the higher education over the years has indirectly made the students to look for alternatives.

External Factors

In the phase of internationalizing higher education,

foreign universities and institutions have been allowed to come into India and establish franchise centers in the country, offering degrees or diplomas, which are not necessarily recognized by the parent universities in their own countries. Indian providers also set up institutions in other countries.

Based on the rates of return analysis, World Bank (1994) focus on basic education, whereas its involvement in higher education is guided by calls for equitable and cost effective financing. It highly favours cost-sharing and the promotion of private higher education to free up scarce public resources for improving basic education. It recommends forcefully that further enrolment expansion in higher education should take place in the private sector. Further, World Bank (2002) indicates that the higher education systems in developing countries and the institutions can only survive if they are flexible for change. The message is clear that the most flexible systems as well as institutions survive and those do not, decay. More differentiated systems, including private and non-university institutions can help meet growing demand and make higher education more responsive to labor market needs. The examples are the successful higher education systems found in Australia and New Zealand other than US. It may also be noted that the European system, perhaps, many of the European countries are undergoing series of policy debates on financing higher education focusing on the extent and degree of cost recovery in higher education for enabling the transition from elite to mass oriented higher education.

To sum up, even though, private institutions offer course on any discipline, the viability and sustainability depends upon their demand. However, it is to be noted that private institutions in developing countries like India are not efficient, competitive and complement as found in developed countries. The absence of a coherent long-term policy perspective on higher education is reflected on the government's ambiguity to regulate private institutions. The unfettered growth of private higher education (especially in engineering and management disciplines) combined with the international economic and political events created a surplus in the labor market in the recent years.

8

Privatization of Higher Education: Dimensions and Challenges

Dr. Abha Singh
Dr. Priya Soni Khare

Privatization of Higher Education is not new concept in India. Higher education has greater and special value in emerging knowledge society. Higher education is one of the important instruments for the best development of human resources. Government is emphasizing for universalization of primary education as well as for the development of secondary education. So in the field of higher sector demand of colleges is less than the required number of institution private sectors came forward to meet the demand.

Privatization is a very broad and developing term. It means very little government involvement and minimum partnerships between government and private service providers. It is the act of reducing the role of government or increase role of private sector. Privatization refers to the shifting of activities, asserts and responsibilities from the government to the private sector.

Some critisized that privatization distorts and distroys the core mission of higher education *i.e.* to seek truth and generate knowledge. But always it is not true. Privatization can cause tremendous social revolution as it is always accomplained by large layoffs.

Normally private higher education funding depends

upon student tuition fee. Private higher institutions have nill government funding support. They manage funds from their own resources. So private higher institutions focus on market forces to shape then students their academic programs as well as their curriculum too. The financial arrangements of private higher institutions offer lack transparency. Numbers of private higher institutions are run only to earn a profit for owners, families or management groups. Government should make and try to implement a strict rules and regulations for these higher institution which should not be violated at any cost.

Need of Privatization

After indepence there has been tremendous expansion of government funded education in our country. But they could not meet the need of society. Indian society is a developing society so education is considered as a tool for social change. Government finds himself unable to meet the demand of higher institution. So government started to encourage privatization of higher education.

Future of Privatization of Higher Education

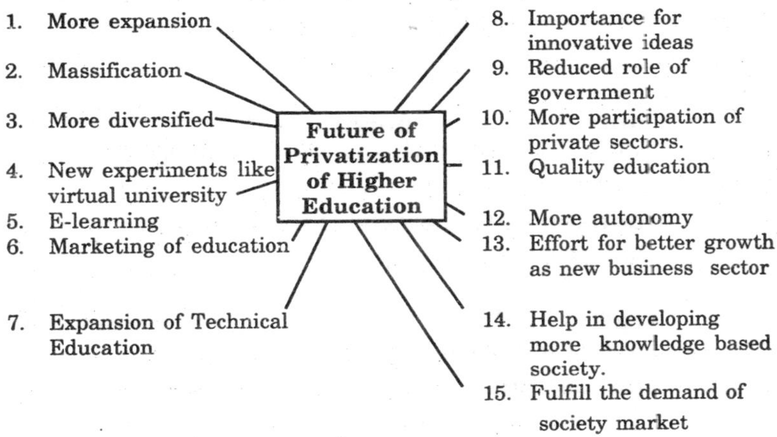

Forces Acting for Privatization

In changing and developing Indian society there are many forces which are forcing privatization. Some major forces are:

1. Quest for higher standard of learning.
2. Increased number of students.
3. Need for today as social requirement.
4. Government limitations for funding.
5. Economic growth.
6. Inflow of private fund.
7. Need for more autonomy.

Dimentions of Privatization

1. Purpose: To develop knowledge and skills for a sustainable future as well as changes in human lifestyle and values.

2. Quality of education: Private institution considers students as a consumer including the concept of the college education as a 'product'. So they believe in proper marketing of institution and to meet the demand which force them to provide quality education. But few new ones are exceptions (poor quality and management).

3. Sources of funds: They have to manage by their own. Student tuition fees is most import way to collect the fund. Private sectors invest in it as future profit means.

4. Ownership: Sometimes a family or group of family or management group acts as owner. The moto of all is to make is a profitable business by providing quality education as per social demand.

5. Control by government: Control by government is very limited and liberal because they do not provide funds to these institutions.

6. Management: Manager of these institutions insure over all management and make co-ordination with concern universities.

7. Staff: Good institutions pay better amount in comparison to public sectors. So they expect better work and more dedication. But in other side few institutions exploit the brain by poor payment.

Challenges of Privalization to Higher Education

Nowadays private institutions are central feature of higher education especially for professional courses (*viz.*B.Tech, MBA, B.Ed. etc.). How to perceive the private institutions and integrate it into the broader academic system in a country and world-wide is a key challenge.

The private institutions will certainly continue to grow and expand in the present higher education market-place. No doubt private institution makes many important contributions. The most important one is providing study opportunities for many students who would not able to find a place at a public institution.

However, the growth of private higher education poses many challenges to higher education system. Few are as under:

1. Public welfare: Most private higher education institutions especially new professional colleges set their rights mainly on their own success and market position rather than their role in a higher education system or in serving the broader public good. They ignore sometimes public needs. Whereas public institutions are regulated by state under strict control and they function as part of a coordinated public system of higher education. How to ensure private institutions to work for public good is a major challenge.

2. Quality assurance: Nowadays quality assurance is one of a major issue in higher education. Private academic institutions focus on market forces to shape their students degree programs and curriculum. To maintain standard of teaching, admission and infrastructure are some aspects which needs the quality assurance. How to maintain these standards is a central issue.

3. To meet international challenges: It is a major challenge in front of private institutions of ensuring that the programs are effectively developed and managed to meet cross border challenges. The private higher education sector's international linkages include franchising, branch campuses and many other programs. The effective development and management of international programs present a challenge that they serve students appropriately.

4. Qualified staff: Many new private colleges depends on part-time teachers with little commitment to the institutions and sometimes with scant qualifications. Many institutions hire teachers from public universities to teach. New private institution rarely focus on research. Teachers are forced to develop market value rather than academics.

Some older private are very good have qualified faculty and appropriate research work and other academic activities. The future of teachers, the role of research and the terms and conditions of academic appointments have all been brought into question by the new private higher education sector.

5. Transparency: Sometimes reliable informations regarding degree offerings and quality is unavailable. Data concerning the effectiveness of academic programs, the success of students in the job market, dropout rates are some times unavailable. They hide due to their market reputation.

6. Funding: With few exceptions, private higher education funding depends largely on students tuition, the financial arrangements of private higher education institutions often lack transparency. In general public resources account for only a small part of funding. Most by private institutions are sources of income for their management group. Collection of funds from right way would be a major challenge in front of higher education system.

Suggestions: At present privatization of higher education especially in the field of professional and technical education (*e.g.* B.Tech, Medical, C.S., I.T. B.Ed, etc.) has already commenced. In the present age of globalization it will neither be appropriate nor practical to check it. But to give better results here are few suggestions:

1. Private universities and colleges should be given recognition by concerning regulating bodies like UGC, AICTE, NCTE and like on the basis of strict norms laid by these bodies to ensure quality and standard of education in them.
2. Admission should be purly on the basis of merit not money even on management seat too.
3. The government should keep strict control over the standard of these institutions.
4. Selection of faculty should be purly on the basis of qualification.
5. The licence permit to open new institution should be given to dedicated individuals having lesser means not to them having more contacts and money. They beat all the hurdles with the help of money and contacts so they try to earn more money only.

6. State should keep control over these institutions for reservation policy and fee structure.
7. Teacher-student ratio should be fixed.
8. It may be a better option to form a local committee of eminent teachers, community leaders, parents, staff members, management members and affiliating university representative to ensure quality and standard and to check monopoly.
9. Good library facility should be there.
10. Research work should be encouraged.
11. Technical universities should involve local industry while developing curriculum.

This will ensure better job opportunity to their students. Industry should provide faculty support in subject areas, where industry has expertise.

Privatized higher education has no doubt great importance in the present edge of globalization and libralization. Public sector institutions are failed to meet the present demand. So we can't overlook privatization of higher education because it is a better option to government as well as students parent too.

References

1. Bhattacharya, G.C. (2003); Teacher Education, Vinod Pustak Mandir, Agra.
2. Chauhan, C.P.S. (2004); *Privatization of Higher Education: A Socio-economic Perspective, University News,* AIU, New Delhi, Vol 42, No. 7.
3. Chauhan C.P.S. (2002) *Higher Education in India challenges of Die Global Trends,* University News, AIU New Delhi, Vol. 40 No. 17.
4. NAAC (2000) *NAAC's Action Plan for Performance Evaluation, Accreditation and Quality up Gradation of College and Universities,* National Assessment and Accreditation Council, Banglore.
5. NAAC (2003), NAAC; *A Profile,* National Assessment and Accreditation Council, Banglore.

9

Role of Privatization in Promoting Higher Education

Mrs. Shika Dhar

Today we are living in 21th century where it is rather far more important at this juncture to look around us and identify a path which can lead all of us to a destination which provides a systematic, harmonious, co-operative and a happy society. The most important tool which we will be needing and using to achieve our desired goal and shape the future is 'education'. Education, right from the preprimary to the university level, should not merely by transmission, acquisition and retention of information but it should be capable of making any person a full person, a holistic person with a pragmatic and positive attitude imbibed with certain values which are cherished by a civilized society. Education is a productive investment. The investment in human capital is one of the major means to accelerate the growth of an economy. In recent years, universities all over the world have been facing a financial crisis, in turn giving birth to many problems associated with it. The problems range from infrastructure to efficiency. If the problem exists even in long run, the developmental issues may be the one in bottleneck.

It seems to be paradoxical that many state financed universities/institutions in our country which were founded with an objective of welfare, on the principle of widening opportunities for higher education for all, are now in a financial crunch. On the other side, the private demand for higher education is increasing, to some extent because of growing unemployment in developing countries. Private education has grown for several reasons, which can be summed up in two categories excess demand and differentiated demand for higher education. First, the social demand for higher education exceeds the public supply, and the private market seeks to meet the unsatisfied demand. Secondly, demand for different quality and content in education also contributes to the growth of privatization. On the supply side private entrepreneurs are ready to provide higher education either for philanthropic or for profit.

Self-financing means the state of freedom and independence in the matter of administration and establishment of the college. The idea of self-financing of higher education stems from the explicit financial difficulties faced by the government in bearing the burden of the colossal system of higher education manned by some 3.1 lakh teachers, their non-teaching counterpart and associated financial implications of teaching. If the productivity of the system howsoever large is commensurate with the cost of running that system, it should not cause much concern. However, when the dead weight of the system is several times larger than its productivity, keeping that system running will necessarily demand support from outside so long as it keeps running. The cause of real concern in the back of minds of the government is the huge deadweight of the system that claims enormous public expenditure without a commensurate meaningful output.

The sphere of higher education is getting wider and wider after independence. There has been an explosion of enrolment in higher education which swelled from less than half a million in 1950-51 to more than one crore in 2004. As on 31 May, 2005, there were 343 universities including 18 Central Universities, 96 Deemed Universities and 13 Institutes of National importance. The government is unable to fulfill the demands of higher education due to mushroom growth of population. So, in this era of privatization the government is making efforts to privatize higher education.

A rapid increase in the number of self-financing colleges has been noticed since 1980s. These institutions meet the everraising demand for professional education specially in the field of medicine technology, management and teacher education, etc. This trend has adversely affected the system of higher education is terms of equity considerations of education since the admissions are based on the principle of ability to pay than on merit. The trend of introducing a large number of self-financing courses at the undergraduate level was substantially encouraged by the introduction of vocational/career oriented courses supported by the schemes of U.G.C.

There is a need to regulate the growth of self-financing courses in higher education institutions. Only those departments in the universities and colleges that have extra staff and expertise may offer some financing courses that may be in demand and not normally offered in the universities. A detailed regulatory framework has to be developed that would allow only genuinely interested private sector that has philanthropy and education and not profit as the main consideration to enter the higher education sector. Tendencies to open profit seeking private institutions need to be curbed altogether, lest higher education be subject to vulgar forms of commercialization.

The need for the expansion of higher education facilities is obvious but it is very important to see that proliferation of poor quality and unviable universities, colleges and other institutions of higher education does not take place. The growth in higher education institutions has to be based on sound criteria. If these institutions establish a healthy and strong process of imparting vocational education through qualified teachers and proper training, then no doubt, the real aim of education can be fulfilled.

References

1. Agarwal, J.C., (2005), *Recent Development and Trends in Education,* Shipra Publications, Delhi.
2. Tilak, J.B.G. (2003), *Education Society and Development, National and International Perspectives,* A.P.H. Publishing Corporation, New Delhi.

10

Privatization of Education and Problem-Solving Skills

Ajay Kumar Singh
Mrs. Nivedita Singh

Education is the most crucial investment in human development. It strongly influences in health hygiene, demographic profile, productivity and practically all that is connected with quality of life. One aspect of globalization is the beliefs that state enterprises should be privatized, since allegedly the profit motive leads to efficiency. Throughout the world this has aroused deep resentment among the workers who see their jobs and their benefits endangered. Even prisons are being turned into for profit institutions, which seems callous. The defunding of public education has resulted in the broad and contested trend of privatization. To advocates, a privatized school system offers the efficiency of a free market rid of bureaucratic bog. To those in opposition, the commercialization of education means inequality and a worsening social plight. As the dispute continues so does the suffering of our public schools.

The Root of the Problem

Theoretically, public education is structured Linder the ideology of equity. Provincial/state government tax revenue is the primary source of funding and legislature dictates mandatory policies and the general curriculum. Similar to other government services, efficient practice is subject to variable social, economic and political factors.

Reports tell that last year's severe economic reforms have drastically impacted school funding. School boards are now forced to cut programs. These and many other prevalent effects of shrinking budgets and decentralized responsibility of public education have created the need for alternative sources.

The Growth of Privatization

Coining it the "privatization of content of education" we can say that the decline of public funding has drastically increased commercial involvement in our schools. "Exclusive marketing, sponsored educational materials, sponsorship agreements, fundraising, and corporate partnerships are becoming further institutionalized. Schools have made major commitments to technology and few, if any, ministries provide the funding. The investment in technology is both a major pressure on school budgets and a significant door for private involvement in schools". Although corporations are supplementing public education, schools offer these companies a virtual monopoly and a major advertising platform to an extremely captive audience, thus allowing corporatization to exist on public time and money. Educationist points out that the result of corporate participation is inequity, as wealthier schools are much more appealing to potential sponsors.

Education as a Mutual Program

Educationist describes how the 'privatization of the structure' has enabled education to become big business. Second in size to healthcare, the global education industry is estimated to be worth $2 trillion, annually. Since the early 1990s 'Educational Maintenance Organizations' have emerged. Convincing school boards that they can run schools more cost efficiently, these private companies are combining education budget money with their own capital and overseeing school operations.

Advocates of these privatization ventures see an opportunity for parents to have choices they deserve, especially in urban school. Appealing to many under funded schools, for-profit education companies are multiplying with revenues. Others argue that the contrast between private and public interests put schools at risk. More responsible to shareholders than students, these organizations may either pull out or sacrifice education for profit.

Problem-Solving

The negative implications of privatization do not erase the circumstances that require it to exist. Experts report that the declining quality of public schools has increased the support of complete privatization. Experts reject any private reform. "To knowingly restructure a public system so that it requires a proportion of those who invest in it to fail for the system to operate correctly is not just, or right, or, frankly, even civilized." But until the government commits to adequate education budgets, the prevention of corporate takeover must be met with alternatives.

Is it possible to restructure a public system that will benefit from private involvement yet maintains the vision of equity and collective good? Implementing laws that have corporations pay taxes instead of benefiting from free advertising and tax breaks and that regulate the management of schools are some suggestions that may offer solutions to this difficult equation.

The objectives of higher education and basic research for any society, particularly one striving to grow into a knowledge society, are not only to address the knowledge needs of the present time, but also to project the knowledge needs of the future, as far as possible. In fact, a knowledge society needs creative minds in the sciences and humanities that are not confined within narrow boundaries set by either the current market trends in the private sector or the policy commitments in the government sector, binding though them may be in the sort run. It is the responsibility of the state to try to determine the futuristic vision with the help of identified groups of knowledge workers, and influence the course of development in pursuit of that vision with appropriate funding.

Conclusion

Privatization is manifestating itself in a variety of forms such as the full recovery of the cost of higher education in government and government aided institutions; high fees in self-financing private processional colleges, deemed and private universities; high fees charged in unrecognized private institutions offering foreign degrees in collaboration with foreign universities etc. Commercialization, therefore, needs to be unambiguously defined with a view to containing it.

A system to regulate privatization should be put in place by the centre and state governments in coordination with each other. If the central government so desires, it may lay down constitutional provisions to regulate commercialization. A suitable framework in respect of specific issues can be imposed by legislation, if necessary, and its implementation may be ensured through various regulatory bodies.

11

Privatization of Higher Education: Perspectives and Challenges

Er. Rahat Khan
Ram Shankar

Introduction

During recent years, private initiative in higher education became almost unavoidable. At the same time, there was increasing pressure in favor of expansion. Since the courts permitted the institutions to charge students in full in certain cases, a large number of new institutions came to be opened. This in turn created a fresh set of problems and all of them have not been taken care of yet. This much is clear by now that the private sector of education has come into existence alongside the governmental sector. One of the problems that need to be taken care of is how the two should co-exist. Secondly, there is the problem of commercialization. Higher education in India is ridden with problems, which are many and various. Some of the most crucial ones that confront us are somewhat controversial and, at any rate, in need of a thorough scrutiny in the overall interest of the country. The issues are, however, inter-dependent and include:

(i) Broadening of access in higher education.
(ii) Ensuring equity in higher education.
(iii) The financial crunch.

(iv) The move to privatize higher education as a remedial measure.

The Important Issues

National Knowledge Commission (NKC) has recently submitted its annual report to the prime minister. The NKC's 'Report to the Nation 2006' states, "destiny of India is in the hands of 550 million people below the age of 25 who will benefit the most from the new knowledge initiatives. The proportion of our population, in the age group 18–24, that enters the world of higher education is around 7 percent, which is only one-half the average for Asia." The NKC therefore recommends creation of "1500 universities nationwide that would enable India to attain a gross enrolment ratio of at least 15 percent by 2015."

The NKC has given recommendations regarding reforms in existing public universities, undergraduate colleges, regulatory structure, financing, quality, creation of national universities as centers of academic excellence and access to marginalized and excluded groups. However, the 'initiatives' or prescriptions provided by the NKC in its report are contrary to the purpose.

There are indications to partially privatize higher education in India as a remedy to most of the problems and issues raised above. The following crucial questions, therefore, need to be consciously raised:

1. What is the rationale for privatizing higher education?
2. What exactly are the issues related to access and equity in higher education and how would privatization tackle them?
3. Will private effort be able to generate the requisite finance for higher education?
4. How has privatization delivered goods in the educational systems abroad?
5. Will private funding of the university system eventually be a substitute to the statutory and constitutional requirement of the State to maintain institutions of higher learning?

6. Will private funding be really available for courses other than those concerned with professional and technical higher education?
7. Will privatization not lead to commercialization?
8. Is commercialization of higher education in national interest?
9. Will privatization not adversely affect interests of the poor and other backward sections of the society?

Access and Equity in Higher Education

India has quite a large system of higher education in as much as we have today 250 universities, over 10,500 colleges and nearly 55 lakhs of students being taught by over 3 lakhs of teachers. And yet the proportion of the university and college going student population in the relevant age group of 16–23 is dismal 6 percent. This is quite low even when compared with developing countries.

On the one hand, we are worried about the so-called 'mushroom growth' of the universities and colleges, and on the other, are unable to provide access to education even at par with most other developing countries in the world. Further, while enrolment of women and those belonging to SC/ST groups and other backward communities has improved, they are still very much under represented. Thus, the twin issue of access and equity needs to be tackled by adopting alternative strategies.

As we all knowns, providing increased access to education, meeting the challenge of equity and improving the quality of education all entail large investment. It is all the more necessary to ensure continuous inflow of funds needed for implementing and carrying out relevant programs and activities. But then there does exist the problem of resource crunch. A suggested way out is exploring additional avenues of generating systems own resources instead of being fully dependent on the State exchequer. It is imperative here that the higher education system has to seek participation both of the government as well as private and voluntary bodies. Some amount of private funding thus appears inevitable for making up the deficit caused by inadequate state funding.

Financial Crunch

Lack of adequate funds in education is the most crucial issue. While overall investment in education as a proportion of the Gross domestic Product (GDP) has gone up from 1.2 percent in 1950s to 3.7 percent in the 1990s, it is still below the norm of 6 percent as stated in the National Policy on Education. University education has particularly been hit hard. Most higher education institutions all over the country are facing acute financial crisis. Two important questions immediately intervene themselves: One, what is the justification for so radically changing the 40-year old policy of state support to higher education, and two, how could the state extend financial support to higher education at a time when the country is facing severe resource crunch?

Since provision of free and compulsory education at the elementary stage is a Constitutional commitment, budgetary allocation for this sector of education is continuously on increase while the university and higher education has got a raw deal for the sixth year in succession. This is in keeping with the declared objective of the Union Government that the lion's share of funding for higher education must come from sources other than the Government. The consequence of inadequate investment in higher education is serious. While the universities are at pain in persuading the government for increased budgetary allocations, some of them have simultaneously taken measures for generating funds of their own.

It is high time the university system resorted to long-term resource planning instead of taking the state support for granted. Each university will now have to identify avenues of resource generation, both internal as well as external, depending upon the nature of its program offerings and the locale. The Punnayya Committee set-up by the UGC and the Swaminathan Panel of the AICTE has made some broad recommendations in this regard. The internal measures, amongst other things, may include proper utilization of funds, general economy in expenditures, pooling and sharing of departmental and institutional resources and most importantly, rationalization of fee structure. As far the external resources, the important avenues include donations from alumni, philanthropists and others, consultancy, university-industry interaction, etc.

In most institutions of higher education, at present, the tuition fees contribute very little towards earnings while the recurring expenditure on each student is much higher. In fact, an upward revision of fees is over due. The need to raise the tuition fees to at least 20 percent of the recurring expenditure per student generally and at a still higher level in higher professional and technical courses is being advocated. Increase in fees from the foreign students at further higher levels is being talked about by reserving seats for them in select institutions like the IIT and the IIMS. While measures such as these appear realistic, their repercussions need to be thoroughly assessed before taking some definite decision in the matter. Particularly, interests of poor students generally and those Indian students who are pitted against the foreign students admitted on the basis of higher fees need to be protected.

By far the least controversial avenue of generating additional resource is that of tapping the philanthropists, alumni and others such as business houses and industrial concerns for voluntary contributions. In order to encourage the Government of India's financial act provides for 100 percent tax exemption in respect of donations by a taxpayer to a university or institution of national eminence. Again, University-Industry interaction is becoming a plank in this direction. The Swaminathan panel has suggested building up a reservoir of funds by collecting educational cess from industries and other user organizations. Setting up of an Educational Development Bank of India initially with shares of Rs. 1000 crore each by the State Governments, Central Government and international financial agencies has also been suggested. Raising money through consultancy work or job assignment by institutions to industries or other professional organizations is yet another avenue being profusely recommended. As an incentive, part of this money goes to individual scholars while the rest is added to the funds of the university. It is pertinent to mention here the official view that avenues generated through enhanced fee structure;

consultancy and other activities would not be offset against Government grants with the industries considering 'adoption' of one or more institutions of higher education.

A major problem in relationship between industry and academia is that perhaps both do not know what the other wants. While the universities are unable to identify the precise needs of the industry, the latter are unaware about the type of interaction universities look forward from them. Could a beginning not be made by sharing the infrastructure each is known to possess?

Privatization of Higher Education in India

The private initiative in education, especially higher education is not altogether new to India. Some of the leading universities namely, the Banaras Hindu University and the Aligarh Muslim University came up with the efforts of certain dedicated individuals and financial support of the community at large. Again, a large number of educational institutions in the country especially those concerned with general and professional higher education have been established on private and voluntary initiative with or without financial subsidy from the Government.

In the context of the current changing social and economic fabric of the country, it appears almost certain to go in for private funding of education. The recent paradigm shift in Indian economic and political philosophy has led to the demand of private universities so as to meet the challenge of contemplated open economy and the demand for qualitative human resources and high level of R&D.

There are views for and against privatization of higher education in India. While some have started criticizing the concept even before it has come to be defined and taken off the ground, others consider it very useful and indeed inevitable. So much so that proposals for setting up private universities affiliating the privately funded institutions are being discussed. For one thing, there is no denying the fact that higher education is comparatively less expensive in India even though under-developed countries like Bangladesh and developed ones like the US, Japan, Australia and many others have successfully switched over to privatization of education without making it a crass. Can India also think on these lines especially if the money earned can be 'ploughed back' into the educational sector for its own improvement?

Summing up, a clear-cut policy of the Government of India regarding privatization of higher education is unfortunately not available at the present moment. We wonder if there is one at all. At any rate, the move is lacking in transparency. One thing is, however, clear from the occasional official pronouncements that there is a need for supplementing government measures by the efforts of the non-government organizations and the institutions themselves to generate resources. This, in a way, does amount to partial privatization calling for caution against, amongst others things the following:

(*a*) Resultant commercialization of education.

(*b*) Obstacles in merit based admissions.

(*c*) Deterioration in academic standards.

(*d*) Encroachment in institutions and autonomy.

(*e*) Service conditions of teachers.

(*f*) Education becoming subservient to market logic advanced by the private sector in the country.

Conclusion

There is an urgent need to evolve a proper co-ordination mechanism amongst the various regulatory bodies in order to determine issues such as fees, admission, procedures, the quality of education, future directions etc. Periodic accreditation of all institutions of higher learning should be made mandatory for the purpose of ensuring quality. It is matter of utmost urgency that each new institution is accredited not later than one year of it being started. In case the relevant professional agencies are unable to meet this demand, these bodies may either be strengthened or some partner agencies with established credibility might be identified and entrusted with the responsibility of carrying out accreditation. Whenever an institution is found in default of the norms laid down by the relevant controlling authority, the latter shall have the right to impose a financial penalty for each default. This should apply to all institutions, including those controlled by the government. The amount chargeable should be laid down in advance at the time of laying down the norms. If an institution more than twice commits the default, the institutions should be debarred from running the courses, as the case might be.

12

Privatization of Education *vs.* Commercialization

Dharmendra Kumar Pandey
Suman Pandey

Introduction

In the present scenario there is drastic change in every concern of society, so education could not be far from it.

As we are all known that several seminar were held and study groups were appointed to discuss about the drastic change in higher education. Privatization of education is a recent phenomenon in higher education. In this present paper some relevant issues has been discussed regarding privatization of education *vs.* Commercialization of education.

Privatization of Education *vs.* Commercialization

The private initiative in education especially higher education is not altogether new to India. Some of the leading universities namely, the Banaras Hindu University and the Aligarh Muslim University came up with the efforts of certain dedicated individuals and financial support of the community at large Again, a large number of educational institutions in the country especially those concerned with general and professional higher education have been established on private and voluntary initiative with or without financial subsidy from the government.

In the context of the current changing social and economic fabric of the country, it appears almost certain to go in for private funding of education. The recent paradigm shift in Indian Economic, and political philosophy had led to the demand of private universities so as to meet the challenge of contemplated open economy and the demand for qualitative human resources and level of R&D.

It is true that higher education is a basic education demanded by the masses but where are the funds needed for such expansion. The resource starved governments are unable to meet this challenge.

The international commission on education for the 21st century in its report entitled, "learning the treasure with in" (1996) suggested that "It is not only justifiable but also desirable to raise money from private sources in order to ease pressure on national budgets, private funding can come from a variety of sources; contributions by families and students towards fees.

In universities and colleges those meritorious students, who could not get admission into state run professional colleges due to limited seats, which were rendered ever more limited due to the application of reservation policies of the government, should not be deprived of the chance of securing a professional education, provided they were ready to meet the expenditure of the course.

Meaning of 'commercialization' is 'exploiting for the purpose of gaining profit'. This commercial approach to privatization of education has led to the establishment of a great number of self-financing institutions, which run professional courses, charging huge amount as capitation fee. It needs to be mentioned that some of these college in India are doing extremely well and providing good infrastructure facilities, competent facility and quality education. Alongside there also exist those institutions which are only concerned with profit earning, with exploiting parents and students rather than providing quality education.

The commercialization of education reinforces existing inequalities as well as creates new disparities. The preparation of any examination needs minimum three lacs of rupees, two years of prime time and is coupled with big uncertainties marked by leaked papers or bogus evaluation.

Many reasons are also found which are favours the privatization of education not commercialization of education.

The Crucial Questions

There are indications to privities higher education in India as a remedy to most of the problems. The following crucial questions therefore need to be consciously raised:

1. What is the rational for privatizing higher education?
2. What exactly are the issues related to access and equity in higher education and how would privatization tackle them?
3. Will private effort be able to generate the requisite finance for higher education.
4. Will private funding of the university system eventually be a substitute to the statuary and constitutional requirement of the state to maintain institutions of higher learning?
5. Will privatization not lead to commercialization?
6. Is commercialization of higher education in national interest?
7. Will privatization not adversely affect interest of the poor and other backward sections of the society?

Suggestion

In privatization of education following suggestions are kept in mind:

1. Private institution needs to become:
   (a) cost effective
   (b) of good quality
   (c) relevant to India's manpower needs and more self-supporting.
2. There is need for restructuring and revitalizing the higher education system to make it more responsive to national need and more self-supportive.
3. The government should formulate a coherent policy, incentive strategy and checks to prevent financial exploitation instead of quality enhancement.
4. There is an urgent need to evolve a proper

coordination mechanism amongst various regulatory bodies in order to determine issues such as fees, admission, procedures, the quality of education, future directions etc.

5. Periodic accreditation of all institutions of higher learning should be made mandatory for the purpose of ensuring quality.
6. Whenever an institution is found in default of the norms laid down by the relevant controlling authority, the latter shall have the right to impose a financial penalty for each default. This should apply to all institutions, including those controlled by the government. The amount chargeable should be laid down in advance at the time of laying down the norms, if an institution more than twice commits the default, the institutions should be debarred from running the courses, as the case might be.

Conclusion

Liberalization and globalization has resulted in a competitive world where communication and technological innovations have resulted in a world without boundaries. Nations in such a world can thrive only on a healthy, literate, well trained and skilled population. Above objective can be fulfill by private, institution. Hence, the Indian Higher Education system in private institution needs to become:

(a) cost effective,
(b) of good quality,
(c) relevant to India's manpower need, and
(d) more self-supporting.

References

1. Abdul Kalam, APJ (2004). *Challenges for Society.* University News, Vol. 42 (37).
2. Khanna, Pratibha (2004). *Financing of Higher Education Private Initiatives in Higher Education: Past, Present and Future.* University News, 42(52).
3. Magazine, *Civil Services Times,* August 2007.
4. Singh, L.C. (2003). *Self-Financing Higher Education,* University News, Vol. 40(52).

13

A Brief Overview of the Private Higher Education System

Ravindra Kumar

Private higher education is not an exception. Private higher education used to exist in many ancient societies largely provided by private individuals and organizations. Private education system existed in India during ancient and medieval periods.

Finance is the most important issue relating to the development of private higher education institutions. It is well recognized that adequacy of finances is a basic necessary condition for development of sustainable private higher education systems. How, why and who finances and how the funds are utilized determines the nature and structure of the private higher education systems while discussing the issues relating to financing private higher education institutions, the need for differentiation between several kinds of private institutions in necessary.

There are various types and forms of private higher education systems and institutions. Here, we discussed university level institutions and colleges. Importantly, recognized and unrecognized institutions. Among the recognized ones also, there are several types: recognized only as institutions fit for importing higher educations, recognized for awarding degrees/diploma/certificates and recognized for financial assistance by state. Lastly, private institutions are of two other types: privately managed and publicly funded, and privately managed and privately funded. Looking at the complexity of the nature and type of 'Private' institutions, a simple definition was given there. Private higher education institutions here:

(a) include both universities and colleges,

(b) they are necessarily privately managed, but not necessarily totally privately funded, and

(c) they are recognized for imparting higher education.

Most of the private higher education institutions in the countries of the region are either aided by the state, or self-financing in nature. While self-financing institutions generally do not received, by definition, any assistance from state, state aided private higher education institutions receive assistance of various types. Government assistance to private higher education institutions towards capital costs is somewhat rare. Even if such assistance is given, it is partial. But most institutions of this category receive assistance towards meeting recurring expenditure; in some cases very high proportions of recurring costs are met by state grants, and in some cases very limited assistance is provided. It is also noted that often-state assistance is only provided a few years after starting the institutions by the private management.

Fees in the state-aided private institutions are also regulated by the government. Generally the fees are equal to the fees in government institutions. But this is with respect to tuition fee and examination fees only. The private institutions enjoy more freedom in the cases of levying several other kinds of fees, like registration fee, admission fee, college development fund, library fee etc.

Most recent approaches of government of this region seem to, however, favour growth of self-financing institutions. These institutions are less regulated by the government, and the role of the government is largely confined to recognition of the institutions as an institution fit for providing higher education, and approval of the syllabus. As these institutions do not receive any financial assistance from the government, they are subject to less rigorous control, and they enjoy considerable freedom in formulating financial policies-in generating revenues and in their spending. Mostly, fees seem to be the single most important source of revenue. Other sources are negligible. Not only recurring costs, even capital costs could be gradually recovered from the students. The allocation of resources, including fixing salaries for teachers and others, is mostly left to those institutions.

In the increasingly globalized systems it is felt that developing countries in the region can learn a few important lessons from the experiences of the developed countries. In developing countries, non-student and non-government sources of finances are negligible in private higher education systems, as they tend to depend upon either government assistance and/or on student fees,, while in developed countries, such as USA, non-student, non-government sources contribute sizable funds for private and even public higher education.

It is necessarily important that state should not abdicate its responsibilities of funding higher education. The recent favorable approach to emergence and growth of private colleges, including more specifically self-financing colleges, is largely based on increasingly worsening budgetary conditions, in relation to allocation to higher education. The level of investment in higher education in many countries of the region is below the required levels, particularly in relation to national income (GNP) and government (federal and provincial) budgets.

Arising Problems

The most important fears, which are being proved true to a great extent, refer to vulgar commercialization of higher education, and playing on the vulnerable conditions of the 'gullible parents', charging exorbitant fees formally and informally, starting from application fee to examination and grade-sheet fees. Students paying exorbitantly high fees obviously do lack any consideration for national interests such as public service, service in rural areas, service of the poor etc.

The second most important problem refers to the insurance of equity in higher edcuation. While the government could do a great extent see that its protective discrimination policies are followed in the private aided college, resistance to such policies is much higher in the case of self-financing institutions.

Thirdly, the government inability to control the quality of education is also being increasingly felt. Generally once recognition is granted to a private institution, and that is not found to be very difficult, the government cannot enforce any of its conditions.

Fourthly, to reduce corruption and ensure fair practices in recruitment of teachers in private aided institutions.

Fifthly, conflicts between national manpower needs and short-term market signals that influence private higher edcuation institutions are found to be serious, which in the long run might produce serious manpower imbalances both shortages and gluts.

All these problems are with respect to 'recognized' private institutions. Emergence of 'fake' universities and ghost institutions imparting higher education and awarding degrees is also a problem that is coming to surface in serious dimensions. As these institutions are not even 'recognized', the role of the government is practically 'nil'.

Occasionally in India, the University Grant Commission or the Association of Indian Universities makes public announcements listing the fake universities and ghost institutions, only to warn the students and parents to be cautious.

Conclusion

Policies with regard to privatize higher edcuation are still in the stage of formulation in this region. The complexity of emerging problems compel the policy planners to quickly find effective solutions. Two kinds of solution are being suggested in this regard. One is: not to allow the growth of private higher education, particularly of a self-financing nature, at all, and rather to close down all such colleges. In the changing socio-economic conditions, this is regarded as an extreme proposal and as impractical. So the alternative approach is to find piece-meal solutions to several problems.

It is increasingly felt that the very rapid growth of a

private self-financing higher education system, in such a short period, might not be desirable and might not even be sustainable in the long run.

Further, from the point of view of finances, it is felt necessary that the resource base of the private higher edcuation systems have to be diversified. Non-governmental, non-student sources of revenues should be exploited, as the whole financial burden cannot be and rather should not be transferred to the students.

Basically the limits to privatise the higher edcuation systems have to be noted. After all, there should be some balance between the private system and size of the public higher edcuation system.

14

Privatization of Higher Education System in India : An Emerging Need

Dr. B. B. Singh
Mrs Sangeeta Singh
Miss Vinita Yadav

"Education is not the amount of the information that is put into your brain and runs riot theme, undigested all your life. We must have life-building and man-making, character-making assimilation of ideas. If you have assimilated five ideas and made them your life and character, you have more education then any man who has got heart a whole library."

—*Swami Vivekanand*

Education is an important index of human development. Being the apex of education pyramid higher education is needed a vital tool for intellectual, cultural and aesthetic development and means for achieving wider social aspirations. It also has an increasingly crucial role to play in producing change agent for moving the country long the development continuum. The phenomena of liberalization and globalization of the Indian economy coupled with revaluation in information technology have brought new challenges to privatization of higher education it is the recent pressing need of society as weli as nation.

The concept of privatization refers to private ownership in varying degrees from total ownership to ownership in the form of joint ventures. The effect of privatization is slowly being felt in all sector of the economy. Inevitably, it is being recommended for the education sector as well. The poor level of resources with the various sectors competing with each other for a share of it has pushed education to a low position on the priority list. The state can no longer cope with situation. Thus more and more people are looking towards privatization of education as a panacea.

This concept refer control and administer of education is managed by individual institution or local bodies and state is completely independent from the responsibilities of education.

Some Facts about Privatization of Education in India

1. In ancient period education : It is completely independent it has been imparted in Gurukul or 'Guru's Ashram'.

2. The regulation act 1813 and wood's dispatch (1854) : It recommended 'zero- privatization' *i.e.* state should be responsible for the education.

3. Indian education commission : It recommended 'policy of withdrawal' of state *i.e.* state should be independent of educational responsibilities.

Needs of privatization: Some facts show the need and importance of privatization in higher education:

1. To reduce financial burden on state : Excessive financial load on state because of two reasons

(a) *High subsidy factor:* 74% of total government responsibility is given to primary education while 19 percent to higher education.

(b) Low Recovery cost of education: Expenditure of education per student is very high while only 5 percent of total cost per student is recovered in the fee income.

2. *Financial crunch:* Financial is shown as below:

(i) UGC has decided to deduct 35 percent of allocated budget from higher education.

(ii) 0.7% of GDP is not adequate for higher education.

3. *Other Reasons for privatization*

(a) *To reduce the effect of caste based reservation:* Due to reservation some times many good students are unable to get admission in good institution. Since privatization does not allow the reservation so it provide a platform for deserving student for their bright future without considering caste crede, colour etc.

(b) *To grow the mutual relationship between higher education and co-operative sector:* In private sector education is directly affected by market force. It prepares the human resources as the demand of market which ensures the dependence of higher education and co-operative sector.

(c) *To improve the quality of education:* Because of ability based selection and requisite allocation of fund to higher education in private sector ensure the improvement the quality of education.

(d) *To access and equity in higher education:* Access and equity in higher education is very low *i.e.* 6 percent only even when compared with developing countries and we have a wide system of higher education system to develop in countries.

Developing country *Name of the country*	% of university student
In Egypt and Thailand	20%
Turkey	10%
Brazil	11%
Mexico	16%

No. of student access to higher education

In developed country	In India
40%	7%

NKC Report, 2006

National Knowledge Commission (MKC) has established by our prime minister Dr. Manmohan Singh on 24 June,

2005. This report has a hidden agenda of privatization. It has given recommendation regarding the reforms in below areas:

1. *The universities* perform a critical role in an economy and society. They create assimilate and disseminate knowledge. Therefore they may must be flexible, innovative and creative.

A suggestion regarding the universities :

(i) Increase the no. of university.

(ii) Continuous internal assessment and reform in annual examination. This expensive suggestion support the privatization.

(iii) NKC's recommendations regarding the reform in the structure of governance of universities.

(1) Independent appointment of V.C., (2) Dispense the large university court, (3) Creation of standing committees of academic council for 'expeditious' decision and (4) V.C. should function as a chief executive officer.

2. *Undergraduate college* NKC Report recommends autonomy to colleges, and these autonomous colleges would constitute a part of 1500 universities by 2015. 200 out of about 17,700 colleges have opted for autonomous status so far and remaining affiliated colleges as a community college.

3. *Regulation:* The NKC proposes the establishment of an independent regulatory authority for higher education (IRAHE) for two reasons.

First entry or letting up of a university through are act of legislature or parliament is a formidable barner.

Second, entry norms will be needed for private institution and public — private partnership. Further it would dispense with the multiplicity of regulatory agencies to provide a single window clearance.

4. *Financing:* The present financial support for higher education at 0.7 percent of GDP. While in an ideal world government support for higher education should be at least 1.5 percent, if not 2 percent of GDP, from a total of 6 percent of GDP for education. But the government should endeavor to reach there level by 2012.

NKC has recommended suggestion for the financial support which are given below:

1. Increase the recovery cost of education: Present recovery cost of education in higher education is 5 percent it should be increased up to 20 percent.

2. Adjustment of fees: Fee should be revised every two years through price indexation.

3. Licensing fees or user charge: To take the charge for facilities in universities used by people from outside.

4. Private investment: It should be encouraged.

5. Quality: To ensure the quality in higher education NKC recommends that,

1. *Same Rule:* All rules that apply to domestic institutions should also be applicable to foreign institutions.
2. *Salary differential salary:* Differential within and between universities as a mean of attracting and retaining talented faculty members.

3. To provide comfortable minimum for all: With some premium for these who perform. This happens in a market model university.

All recommendations are the base for privatization.

6. National universities: In order to increase the gross enrollment the, NKC recommends the creation of up to 50 national universities that can provide education of the highest standard.

7. Access: Economy barriers to higher education be address according to the report by scholarship or cross subsidies.

The NKC proposes 'Deprivation Index' rather than reservation.

NKC reports and privatization: The entire structure of higher education in India presented in the NKC's report to the nation 2006 is elitist and will not benefit the vast majority of young people below the age of 25 years it will decrease the enrolment instead of raising it to 15 percent by 2015. Raising the student fees to 20 percent of the recurring expenditure, financing pattern, private investment, salary differential, regulation by IRAHE with enormous powers, bias against the disadvantaged section of the society, autonomous colleges, elitist national universities based on commercialization cleared to privatization and commercialization of higher education in India.

Consequences of privatization: Consequences of privatization can be discussed under the point of advantages or disadvantages.

Disadvantages

1. ***Expensive education:*** The institution run by the private management make a fast back by marketing there courses and collecting huge sums of money by way of donation and capitation fees and at the same time charging hefty fees.

2. ***High recovery cost of education*** in an ideal government conditions the recovery cost in higher education should be 20 percent but in privatization 100 percent is recovered from the student.

3. ***Education as profit making:*** Privatization in higher education makes the education as profit – making rather to human making nourishment of creativity, incalcation of human values, character – building all these aim of educat ion is adversely effected.

4. ***Excessive competition:*** Privatization leads excessive competition for the students while we knows competitions is good only for the intelligent *i.e.* high IQ not for average and below average students.

5. ***To oppose the public conservation law:*** Privatizaticn is against the public conservation law of higher education and it support the economical exploitation.

Advantage of Privatization

1. ***To reduce the workload on state:*** Due to the Privatization state become free from the educational responsibilities which lighten its workload.

2. ***To reduce the financial burden on state:*** The recovery of total cost per student of education from student would facilitate withdrawal of state subsidies and light the burden on the state.

3. ***To improve the quality of education:*** Privatization by getting back the whole cost of education, or a large percentage of it, by way of education fees, donation, would instill greater responsibility in the student. The student in

turn, would take greater interest in ensuring an improvement in the quality of education.

4. *Reduce the crowed in the higher education:* Because of the expensive education only those student who takes the future in higher education would like to go in this field which check the crowed in higher education.

5. *Improve the quality of education:* In privatization institutions would be favored with greater freedom they would be able to hire talented staff, paying them better salaries see these helps to improve the quality of education.

6. *To strengthen the mutual relationship between corporate sector and higher education:* Privatization will also urge the beneficiaries of the output of educational establishments mainly the corporate sector provide the fund while institution produce the student according to their needs. This reduces the problem of educated unemployment.

7. *Facilitate the globalization and foreign currency:* Privatization ensure the quality of education and qualitative education attract the foreign students in our institution which facilitate the globalization and it also helps to gain the foreign currency.

Conclusion

The developing countries like India where 97 percent *student wants to join higher education the zero-privatization is not possible.* Zero-privatization is not success and in the present condition the privatization of education has emerged as a panacea in financial problem. But in Indian society, where the aim of education is the all round development of personality, the higher education can't merely a vocational approaches. A clear cut policy of India regarding the privatization of higher education is unfortunately not available at the present moment. So we are not in the state to accept it completely. Therefore, there is a need for implementing government measures by the efforts of the non-government organization and the institutions themselves to generate resources. As a researcher I think that the partial privatization is the better option for us.

References

1. Anand, C.L., *Privatization of Higher Education in India: Rational and Perspectives,* 1-4.
2. Patil, V.K., *Employment News,* 12-18, Oct., 2002.
3. *11th Fifth Year Plan Budget,* 2007-08.
4. *Yozana,* 2002.
5. *Education: The Emerging trends,* DEI magazine (2004-05); (32, 41, 71-72).
6. *National Knowledge Commission* REPORT, 2006.
7. *Yojana,* May, 2007.

15

Self-Financed Teacher Training Institutions: Issues Related to Professional Quality

Dr. Alka Rani

Education is a process of human enlightenment and empowerment for the achievement of a better and higher quality of life. The aim of higher education is to help the students to develop their intellectual, aesthetic, emotional, moral and spiritual temperament and capacities. Therefore, higher educational institutions play a vital role in national development.

Institutionalized education system is of relatively recent origin in India. Though Indian tradition has fostered learning in general, the modern Indian higher education institutions–universities and colleges are patterned after the 19th century British universities. As there were no big private individuals or groups with enough resources to invest on higher education, the then rulers established and maintained the few universities with the public funds. In 1882, however, the Government of India appointed Hunter Commission that advocated among other things, the gradual withdrawal of the state from the direct support and management of these institutions. That was the first indication of the government's resolve to leave higher education to private initiatives. However, some more universities were established but under both public and private support through appropriate legislations due to certain exigencies based on the Education Policy of 1913. (As quoted by Gnanam, 2004, p. 107)

After getting independence, the constitution declares India a sovereign, socialist democratic republic and to secure to all its citizens, justice, liberty, equality and fraternity. These four basic principles are the foundation-stones of educational policy in India after Independence. Education is a state subject. Entry II of the List II of the seventh schedule of the Constitution says: "Education including universities, subject to the provisions of entries 63–66 of List I and entry 25 to List III should be a state subject.(As quoted by Pandey, R.S., 1992, p.38)

Before 1976, education was the exclusive responsibility of the states. The Central Government was only concerned with certain areas like co-ordination and determination of standards in technical and higher education. In 1976, through the 42nd Constitutional Amendment education was incorporated to the Concurrent List and it became ajoint responsibility of the Centre and the states. (As quoted by Shaikh Saleem, 2003, p.5)

By early 1980s, the governmental resource for education reached its limit, the trend of globalization was increasingly visible and the influx of private providers began to establish the self-financing colleges. Virtually all the institutions started after early 80s are private ones except for one or two universities in the states that too only to manage the academic regulation of the increasing number of colleges under the affiliating system. (As quoted by Gnanam, p.108)

Nowadays, the mushroom growth of higher educational institutions has compelled to think over the quality of higher education. As of now the mission of private higher education in India seems to capitalize the demand for higher education in some selected areas for profit.

Professional courses are being started in self-financing institutions for making-money. Admission based on capitation fee are tantamounted to commercialization of education. Thus, self-financing higher education institutions have become a place where money power replaced the merit of the students. This has violated the basic concept of equity as has been enshrined in the Indian Constitution (Articles 14–6). The problems in getting admission in reputed government funded institution compels the students to take admission in Self-financing institutions. Teacher training is also a professional course and preferred by the students. There is a great responsibility of teacher training institutions to maintain the quality because teachers are the trail-blazers of learners and can contribute their utmost in the national development.

Quality and social relevance of higher education in self-financing institutions is deteriorating day-by-day. There are certain issues on which we have to thinkover so that the quality of teacher training institutions may be maintained:

1. Inequity: Government of India has paid attention towards the education of socially disadvantaged groups and other weaker sections of the society. Now, when they moved towards higher education, the government instead of welcoming them for higher education decided to cut down subsidy on higher education.

The system of self-financing trend is increasing the gap between the rich and the poor, suppressing the very basic spirit of our constitution. Growth without equity increases structural disequilibrium, perpetuates poverty, which is itself a constraint to growth.

2. Inadequate infrastructural facilities: It seems that in self-financing institutions, infrastrutural facilities are not appropriate such as: space and building, equipment, books and journals, furniture, etc.

It has been observed that although the infrastrutural facilities are not adequate in self-financing teacher training institutions, they get recognition from NCTE. A question arises while observing such type of teacher training institutions that how the NCTE give recognition to such self-financing institutions and a question mark raised about the functioning of the NCTE.

3. Lack of trained teachers/staff: Sometimes it seems that in self-financing institutions, there is lack of trained professionals/teachers. Teachers do not fulfil the criteria and their number is limited. Whereas, in teacher training institutions there should be teachers of all subject areas.

Teachers are not acquainted with the emerging new technologies so they are not capable to provide current information.

4. Problems related to Practice teaching: Ideally the teacher training institutions have model schools but none of the self-financing teacher training institution has it. The number of the practicing schools is also limited so the purpose of practice teaching is not achieved (served).

Generally the students are not regular as it reflects in the observation of final lesson plans and their teaching style.

5. Pressure of local persons: In teacher-training course, students and parents are eager to get admission somehow and after getting admission they pressurise the teachers to get good marks in practical as well as theory. Perhaps, they think that money and pressure can purchase every individual.

6. Diversion of aim: Nowadays, students are not serious about any profession. Their aim is to get the degree and earn money as soon as possible by hooks or crooks.

It has been observed that the students who obtained their entry into self-financing institutions on the basis of money power show less interest in their studies because of low IQ level they find it difficult to understand the course content. They know that with their money power it will not be difficult to manipulate the examination results. After all for private institutions, money is everything. They are least bothered about the quality of the products.

7. Unfair practice in admission: It is bitter truth that some administrative persons are also indulged in the unfair practice of admission process.

8. Deterioration in values: Value inculcation is the prime need of any society or nation but these institutions are creating distances and feelings of superiority and inferiority because the message is going among students that their merit has no value, only money is supreme and so meritorious students are feeling embarrassment in the society.

Co-curricular activities are the part of teacher training course and values can be inculcated through it. But students are not regular and the staff is limited, so the aim of cocurricular activities can't be achieved.

In the emergent scenario, the major thrust is on quality education. Whenever, we talk about quality education it becomes necessary to review the functioning of whole system. We can't deny this fact that due to not providing financial assistance by the state, the quality of self-financing teacher training institutions is deteriorating day-by-day. The self-financing teacher training institutions are indulging in earning money. The administrators are not serious about the quality of the institutions. The recommendations of various commissions and committees also reflect that providing quality education is the responsibility of state.

The Radhakrishnan Commission (1949) recommended for strengthening the economy of universities that: *(i)* The state must accept its responsibility of providing financial aid to higher education; *(ii)* The government should provide additional grants wherever necessary; and *(iii)* A grants commission should be appointed for determining the grants to be given to educational institutions. (As quoted by Bhatnagar and Saxena, 2001, p. 242).

The Kothari Commission stated that sectors of education which have a multiplying effect like post-graduate studies or teacher education or those which tend to decrease wastage or intensify utilization, there is urgent need to examine continually the relationship between cost and quality and to develop programms which would obtain the highest possible quality for a given level of input. The commission recommended that the UGC should provide financial support for the development of such studies in a few selected universities and that a similar program for the school stage should be developed in the NCERT and the State Institutes of Education.

The Government of India should make provision of funds in the centrally sponsored sector to assist state government to assist state governments to develop teacher education, which is now outside the universities. (The Report of "The Education Commission, 1964-66: Education and National Development, 1966").

In 1967, Committee of Members of Parliament on education recommended that each state should prepare and implement, on a priority basis, a plan for the expansion and improvement of teacher education at all stages.(NCTE document, 95/4, 1995, p. 32)

The working group for preparing a scheme for Revitalization and Modernization of the Pre-Service Teacher Education 1986 (NCERT) recommended that the state Government should provide full financial support to all teacher training institutions in the state so as to provide the minimum facilities. (Aggarwal, J.C. 'Teacher Education Theory and Practice', p. 87)

Programme of Action (1986) recommended that each state government will set-up immediately a task force for making an assessment of the number of institutions. The task force will identify the existing institutions which can be developed as District Institutes of Education and Training (DIETs). Central government will meet a major share in funding. (NCTE document: Policy Perspectives in Teacher Education, p. 39)

The Justice Punnaya Committee, appointed by UGC in 1992 to look into the problem of resources for higher education. The committee found that higher education is primarily a state responsibility. (As quoted by Singh, R., p.10)

The UNESCO document (1995) clearly undermines the socio-economic importance of higher education when it states–"State and society must perceive higher education not as a burden on federal budgets but as a long-term domestic investment in order to increase economic competitiveness, cultural development and social cohesion. The Rastogi Committee also recommended that higher education should be funded largely by the State. (As quoted by Singh, R., p.10)

Suggessions

Constitution of India imposes responsibility on the centre and states to facilitate education to all. UGC should financially support the universities and colleges for improvement of university education. Governments of respective countries should provide adequate resources for higher education.

The government is trying to shift the burden of college expenditure of salaries and non-salaries on public by enhancing fees under Educational Institutions Regulatory

Authority (ETRA). It reflects that the poor public will be deprived of higher education as they will not in a position to pay the increase fees. Higher education will be an education of the rich and poor will be denied higher education. Self-financing institutions are profit oriented, with little consideration for national manpower needs, which may cause serious imbalance in the manpower in the economy.

To maintain the quality of self-financing TTIs–*(i)* The representatives of the NCTE should inspect the self-financing teacher training institutions at least once in each session. *(ii)* NCTE should take hard steps to regularize the session of all teacher training institutions. *(iii)* NCTE should try to maintain uniformity in the time schedule for admission in all teacher training institutions. *(iv)* At the time of admission in teacher training institutions, NCTE should publish the list of self-financing recognised institutions and courses in the newspapers so that the students may not remain in dark. *(v)* The NCTE should ensure timely circulation of the Journals/ Monthly magazines! Newsletters to appraise the Self-Financing teacher training institutions of the prescribed nonns. *(vi)* The NCTE should provide latest literature related to education to the self-financing teacher training institutions from time-to-time. *(vi)* The representative nominated by NCTE should supervise the practice teaching in all the self-financing teacher training institutions. *(vii)* NCTE should recognize only those self-financing teacher training institutions which have the model schools for practice teaching. *(viii)* NCTE should direct all the self-financing teacher training institutions to give more attention to the evaluations at the time of practice teaching. *(ix)* NCTE should direct the self-financing TTIs that the supervision of lesson plans should be done by the concerned subject teachers. *(x)* NCTE should inspire to the self-financing teacher training institutions for maximum use of modern technology. *(xi)* NCTE should give information about their seminars, workshops, competitions, etc. in the newspapers for more participants of teacher-educators/student teachers.

To reduce the pressure of local persons, it is recommended that the students of one region should be admitted in self-financing institutions of other region.

It is necessary to maintain the ratio of demand and supply. Only the devoted persons towards teaching profession should be get admitted.

It is necessary to develop competencies among teachers and students of self-financing institutions. Values may be inculcate only through ideal actions. So the verbal and non-verbal behavior of teacher educators should be imitable. It becomes better if the teacher-educators get in-service training.

Infrastructural facilities should be provided so that the teaching-learning process run smoothly. Use of modern technology undoubtedly may be helpful in upgradation of quality of TTIs. Generally, different departments of the same university hesitate to share the costly equipment like Xerox machine, projectors, computer labs, libraries and internet facilities. Sharing will definitely reduce the expenditure of each university.

In India, there is a need to ensure the assess and equity for masses in higher education. No doubt that majority of people who are benefiting from higher education belongs to the upper socio-economic background, but now the poor too have started achieving higher education. At this juncture, we cannot stop the entry of these talented and creative people only because of their lower SES. It is the responsibility of government to provide opportunity for these people to receive higher education so that they may make original contribution in making India a developed country. Provision of educational loans at low rates of interest to students should be available.

The people who are spending thousands and lakhs of rupees to get a degree of a particular profession will definitely exercise their influence and money in securing a seat of employment. It is happening nowadays and will continue in future too, as the steady and continuous deterioration of values of life. Again the sufferers are the meritorious and talented students particularly those who belonged to the low SES background. Thus the talent and creative abilities may not be utilized for development programs of the country. It will be a great loss to the nation.

Our former president Dr. A.P.J. Abdul Kalam also stated that Government's support should be available in empowering management agencies in providing initially, economic support and finding the right type of management structure and the leaders to manage. (Convocation Address delivered at the 21st convocation of Ranchi University, Ranchi on 13th Feb., 2004)

References

1. Aggarwal, J.C. (1998), 'Teacher Education Theory and Practice,' Published by Doaba House,1688, Nai Sarak, Delhi, p. 87.
2. Bhatnagar, S. and Saxena A, (2001), 'Modern Indian Education and its Problems' Published by Surya Publications, Near Govt. Inter College, Meerut, pp. 244-245.
3. Convocation Address delivered at the 21st convocation of Ranchi University, Ranchi on 13th Feb., 2004 as quoted in University News, Vol. 42, No. 44, Nov., 01-07, p.19, published by S. Chand & Comp. Ltd.,7361, Ram Nagar, New Delhi.
4. Gnanam A.(2004), 'Privatization in Relation to Globalization in the Indian Context'; article published in *University News,* Vol. 42, No.7, Feb., 16-22, p.107-108 published by S. Chand & Comp. Ltd.,7361, Ram Nagar, New Delhi.
5. *NCTE document 95/4 Policy Perspectives in Teacher Education,* New Delhi.
6. Pandey, R.S. (1992), 'National Policy on Education in India, Horizon Publishers, 11/6, Darbhanga Castle, Allahabad, p.38.
7. Saleem Shaikh (2003), 'Privatization of Higher Education' article published in University News, Vol. 41, No. 28, July 14-20, p.5, published by S. Chand & Comp. Ltd.,7361, Ram Nagar, New Delhi.
8. Singh, R. (2005)—'Privatization of Higher Education in the Era of Globilization' article published in *University News,* Vol. 43, No.34, August 22-28, p.10, published by S. Chand & Comp. Ltd.,7361, Ram Nagar, New Delhi.
9. The Report of 'The Education Commission' 1964-66, Educational and National Development, Ministry of Education, Govt. of India, New Delhi, 1966.

16

Mushroom Growth of Higher Educational Institutions and Quality Control

Dilip Kumar Tiwari

Introduction

Higher education occupies a significant position in educational system of a nation because it is the apex of entire educational structure and influences all levels of education.

Formal beginning of university system in the modern sense started in 1857 in India with the launching of three Presidency Universities in Bombay, Calcutta and Madras. This was prompted by the significant Charles Wood's despatch of 1854 to the then Governor-General in India. At that time, the aim was to create a cadre of English knowing clerical cadre to serve the colonial rule of British India. This Indian University system with colonial rootings, started off, with a limited objective of creating a clerical cadre and not to speak of laudable objective of higher education, *viz.*, knowledge creation and knowledge dissemination.

Status of Higher Education in India

Since independence higher education has grown in the country substantially. Now, there are approximately 36 universities, 18,000 colleges, within estimated 106 lakh students enrolled in the higher education institutions. Merely increasing the number of higher educational institutions and their enrolment capacity will not achieve the national development goals without concurrent attention to quality of the educational system, its access to those who desire, and equity measures ensuring fair and impartial treatment of the disadvantaged sections of the society.

The Indian higher education system in its vastness is the second largest after America. In spite of and impressive quantitative expansion, India lags behind developed nations and also some of the developing nations in regard to access to higher education. The enrolment ratio in higher education is about 100 percent in Canada. 80 percent in USA, 50 percent in France and 30 percent in UK. Where as, our higher education hardly covers six percent which is lower than even that of Indonesia (11 percent), Brazil (12 percent), Thailand (19 percent). Out of total enrolment, 46.1 percent of students are marts, 19.9 percent in Science, 17.8 percent in Commerce and management, 1.3 percent in education (Teacher Training and shasri), 6.9 percent in engineering, 3.1 percent in medicine, 0.6 percent in agriculture, 0.2 percent in vet. science, 3.2 percent law, 0.9 percent in others viz., music, drawing painting library science, physical education, journalism, social work etc. (UGC, Information and Statistics Bureau, 2003).

Progress and Prospects of Higher Education in India

The progress and prospects of higher education in India are assessed from different angles. The all India growth of students enrolment in India for higher education from 1983 to 2002-03 is depicted in the Table 15.1.

Table 16.1 : Growth of Students Enrolment for Higher Education in India (2002-03)

Year	*Total Enrolment*	*Increase over the preceding Year*	*Percentage*
1983-84	3307689	174556	5.6
1984-85	3404096	96447	2.9
1985-86	3605029	200933	5.9
1986-87	3757158	152129	4.2

1987-88	4020159	263001	7.0
1988-89	4285489	265330	6.6
1989-90	4602680	317191	7.4
1990-91	4924868	322188	7.0
1991-92	5265886	341018	6.9
1992-93	5534966	269080	5.1
1993-94	5817249	282283	5.1
1994-95	6113929	296680	5.1
1995-96	6574005	460076	7.5
1996-97	6842598	268593	4.1
1997-98	7260418	417820	6.1
1998-99	7705520	445102	6.1
1999-00	8050607	345087	4.5
2000-01	8399443	348836	4.3
2001-02	8821095	421652	5.0
2002-03	9227833	406738	4.6

*Provisional source:*www.ugc.ac.in

Progress and prospect of any country depends on the growth and development of higher education. Hence higher education in very essential for the proper use of human and other natural resources for the development and growth of Indian economy. However, it is not possible to utilize the abundant natural and resources properly due to lack of basic infrast and low investment in higher education. I investment in higher education is not only low I inconsistent in growth. Therefore, there is and urge to hike the investment in higher education from 3.2 percent of the GDP to seven to eight percent GDP to make it competitive and at par with inter higher education in the gloabalized scenario.

Self-Financing of Higher Education and its Quality Control

Ours is third largest system of higher education in the world. In the year 2002-03 we were having 356 institutions imparting education or conducting research in the field of higher education. This figure is now more than 356. The enrolment in these institutions was about 106 lakhs. It is worth here that in India, enrolments in higher education constitute hardly six percent of the age group population, which is very low as compared to 20-25 percent enrolments in advanced countries.

Like any other country in the world, higher education in India is an important sector of national life. Because of large size of higher education (due to its population), huge amount of financial resources are required in running this system to the reasonable satisfaction of all concerned with higher education. During last 10 years in general and 5 years in particular, the focus of government has been shifted from higher education to primary education. This is primarily due to the policy framework of the international agencies like World Bank and UNESCO. Investment (in the form of financial assistance of grant in aid) in higher education is now being weighed in terms of social and private returns in higher education is less than return in primary education. This is why many countries in the world have started reducing the government subsidy for higher education and have encouraged private bodies to come forward and to fill in the gap. Consequently private sector has come in a big way to establish, finance and manage institutions of higher education in general and professional education in particular.

We are not yet accustomed to the concept of 'privatization' of 'self-financing' of higher education to digest. It is our general perception that by allowing establishment of privately or self-financing institutions or courses in higher education, the government has somehow encoached our right to get subsidised higher education. We deliberately try to forget the fact that since the beginning of the humanity, educational institutions have been opened and managed by individuals or private bodies. The term privatization has been used in terms of managing or administering an institution—be it industrial or educational and not financing of institution as such. It is, however true that till few years back, almost 90 percent of the expenditure of higher educational institutes were borne by the government through grant-in-aid or matching grant. Due to out of control population growth and consistently growing enrolment in higher education. The government is regularly withdrawing from the field of higher education underdictate from international bodies like Word Bank, IFC, etc. At the same time, one should also know the fact that there is financial crunch at the government level due to poor or mismanaged policies and schemes and very low economic growth rate. The Constitution of India clearly and specifically directs the government (both central and state) to fulfil the social commitments towards poor and have-nots, for which huge amount of money is required and hence the drastic cut in financial assistance to higher education.

The concept of self-financing institutions was pioneered by Dr. T.M. Pai, who advocated the establishment of well equipped and quality driven institutions of higher learning at places where colleges were few and ill equipped. Initially these types of institutions were established in the field of professional education *i.e.* Medical, Engineering Management along with complete infrastructure facilities and quality measures at the places where there is no such colleges or very few colleges. The fee charged in these institutions. Even then Dr. Pai earned a good name in the field of education. Soon these institutions become so much famous and prestigious that every meritorious and wood-working student from every part of the country was willing to get admission there. These institution is were not the centre of criticism or cry at that time as is the case today. The success of these institutions knocked the ears of some 'ambitious but opportunist people' in association with politicians throughout the country. This led to the opening of not only professional institutions but also general higher educational institutions throughout the country. The shift in government policy to lay emphasis on primary education acted as a catalyst in government policy to lay emphasis on primary education acted as a 'catalyst measure' in opening of these self-financing institutions in the field of higher education.

We shall now concentrate our discussion on the term 'quality' educationists have borrowed various terms and concepts from industry. Quality is also one such concept 'Quality' is usually defined as the totality of features and characteristics of higher education which both institutions imparting higher education and individuals having received higher education should reflect. It is true that higher education in free India has grown tremendously in terms of quantity. However, it is also true that higher educational institution in general and individuals (who have received higher education) in particular have been lacking the various quality measures. It is generally perceived and observed that most of the institutions imparting higher education today lack in terms of:

(a) Infrastructure facilities like building, library, laboratory, equipment playground, furniture, etc.
(b) Level and standard of education, they are imparting.
(c) Fulfilling the needs and requirements of the society.
(d) Competiting their counterparts in global world.
(e) Willingness to adapt for change.
(f) Developing leadership qualities among its product.
(g) International comparability of standard, etc.

The agony is that neither teachers in these institutions are satisfied with their job nor the product of these institution (*i.e.* students) because of obsolete, outdated, irrelevant, unproductive and theoretical knowledge they are receiving. It is not that only self-financing institutions are the centry of such criticism but government aided or funded institutions are also sailing in the same boat. How then, self financing institutions alone are to be blamed for detoration in quality of education? If we recall our activities in various fields of like, we shall be able to note that we prefer our wards to get preprimary/primary/secondary education from self-financing (private or public or convent) schools; we prefer to buy a product of private multinational company over government company; even we prefer to send our mails through private courier over post office. The list is incomplete and its purpose is to say that if privatization or non-government efforts are concerned, it is only higher education which has come under criticism from various quarters of the society. This leads us to conclude that we are not fair or objective in our approach. This also leads us to think that we are running blindly without seeing the reality. To me, reality is that there is a wide difference between the fee charged in these two types of institutions reality is that the proprietors of these institutions are minting money from these institutions and they do not spend money even on essential requirements of the institutions; reality is that inspite of clear cut provisions (rules and regulations) the management of these institutions do not recruit qualified teachers and do not pay full pay to the teachers; reality is that service conditions (including work culture) of the employees in these in these institution are not up to the mark as compared to their counterparts in government funded institutions and the like.

As stated above, the increasing pressure of enrolment of students aspiring higher education and shift in government policy to give more emphasis to primary education over higher education has given rise to opening of higher education institution without government financial assistance. We have to accept this reality. We can only aspire that these self-financing institutions should fulfill the needs of requirements of individual and society. By adopting certain measures.

1. The fee of government aided or funded institutions should be increased substantial.
2. The teacher's job satisfaction is an important factor of quality measure. Therefore, teachers of self-financing institutions should be paid equal emoluments as their counterparts receive in aided institutions.
3. The teacher of self-financing institutions must posses the same qualification as prescribed by UGC/State Government. A sub standard teacher can only produce a sub-standard student.
4. The proprietors of self-financing institutions should feel that running an educa tional institution is not a commercial venture. They owe certain responsibility towards society.
5. The poor (and have not) students in self-financing institutions should be given scholarships to meet their expenses.
6. Meritorious students of these institutions should be charged lower fee irrespective of their income level.
7. The government should permit opening of self-financial institutions only in the areas where there is no for few institutions to fulfill the educational needs of the area.
8. Some types of mechanism of check and balance should be developed and employed with full transparency.

References

1. Bates, R. (2005), *On the Future of Teacher Education Challenges,* Context Content, Journal of Education of Teaching, Manchester.
2. Periyasamy, P. and Venkatesh, J. (2004), *Globalization of Higher Education Means for India,* University News 42 (40).
3. Niladri Pradhan Research Scholar, U.G.C. (Net) Regional Institute of Education, N.C.E.R.T), Bhubaneswer.
4. Thangamuthu, C., Vice Chancellor, Bharathidasan University Tiruehirappalli.
5. Shirvalshetti, A.S., Faculty Member, P.G. Department of Commerce, Karnatak University P.G. Centre Kodi Bagh, Karwar-581303, Progress and Prospects of Higher Education in India.
6. Indian Journal of Educational Research, Vol. 22, No. 2, July-Dec. 2003.
7. Dr. S.C. Agrawal, Reader, Dept. of Education, C.S.J.M. University Kanpur, Self-Financing in Higher Education and its Quality.

17

Privatization of Education: Looking Back and Thinking of the Future

Kuldeep Singh Tomar
Dr. R.K. Panday

Privatization is a complex phenomena with very little government involvement and encouraging private service providers does minimizing the partnership between both with gradual transfer for financial responsibilities from the government to private sectors.

The concept of privatization is not new to education sector in India. Privatization was dominant before British period and was managed completely by individuals belonging to a certain class. The rulers or the government financed education through donations and endowments, but never interfered with its management and routine functioning.

The first-three modern universities were established at Calcutta, Bombay and Madras in 1847. Since independence in 1947. India was witness a tremendous expansion in professional education especially in engineering, medicine and management.

Now India has 291 universities of which 70 are deemed universities, 17 Central, 151 States, 40 Agricultural, 33 Engineering and Technical, 18 Medical, 18 Languages, 9 open and 5 are women's universities.

UGC deals the universities and colleges and MIC. deals

medical colleges in India. The government should exercise some control over the standards of these private institutions through a policy of accreditation. Private institutions should be given recognition on the basics of norms laid down by U.G.C., AICTE, NCTE, MCI to ensure the quality and standars of education. The National Assessment and Accreditation Council (NAAC) is doing a good job. But still lots move have to be done is assessment of the colleges.

In the context of education quality refers to the features of education which was the satisfy the needs of students, parents and the society at large by developing appropriate knowledge and skills. In the Indian context privatization is not suitable as majority of population lies below poverty line and do not have the means and access to education. Our aim is not to educate the elites only but the masses. The privatization will hidden the socio-economic gulf and would go against the constitutional obligation of providing equal opportunities of education to all at different levels. So, a step towards complete privatization of professional education is towards commercialization in future.

References

1. Ambani, Mukesh 2000: *Report on a Policy Framework for Reforms in Education.* Govt. of India, New Delhi.
2. Azad, J.L. : *Privatization of Higher Education,* University News, Vol. 42 No. 7 Feb., 2004.
3. Tilak, J.B.G. (1999) : "Privatization of Higher Education," Vol. 21, No. 2 (1999).
4. UNESCO, 1995 : "Policy Papers on Change and Development in Higher Education", Paris.

18

Self-Financing: Genesis and Role in Empowerment

Dr. Chandresh Kumar Singh
Ritesh Barnawal

Higher education aims at promoting excellence through knowledge generating process with social justice. Higher education affects each and every level of student by producing manpower for each level as well as for many other human endeavor. Higher education is supposed to remain critic of culture and society. Also, it creates the new culture by directing the social change towards positive and healthy direction. Higher education tries to achieve attributes of modernity like Information Technology, Media etc. It also helps to break the shackles of moors and orthodox traditions. By providing manpower to many fields in the society, higher education, thereby plays vital role in the quality living and life of people. In other words, higher education is crucial for healthy society, increased production, better planning and management, research and development and communication. Owing to importance of higher education in one's life, higher education must reach to poorest of the poor in remotest of the remote area so that every member of society is better equipped to have honour of contributing for his or her own welfare and capable of bringing development for his society.

Education earlier was restricted to few individuals, and

a small section of the society. Only an elite group had the luxury to get education. But today is the era of 'Education for all'. Every individual has to be educated. Government efforts and resources for our country proves insufficient due to enormity in population and lack of resources. Here inception of self-financing institutions took place. One should be realistic while having vision of higher education for all.

Privatization, liberalization and globalization entered in India in 1990's concept of self-finance took birth with the repercussions of trinity of privatization, Liberatization and Globalization. But the question arises, do self-financing institution have better inputs and outputs? Are they providing quality education to our young once? What is quality of their intake? Are teachers qualified and are paid enough? Do they have good infrastructure? When these questions would be asked for majority of self-financing institutions, the answer would be 'no'. May be that there are few exceptions. Exceptions can lead the population but cannot represent the population. So our generalizations would base on the majority not exceptions.

When we come to output, still the picture is not glowing one. Output of students when compared to regular ones are poorer one due to poor input. Candidates from regular institutions are way ahead when competed in job market. Most of the MNC's and NC's demand for that regular output having brand name. So seeing the number of self-financing institutions and their large number of output what we are finding that a major section of our population are deprived of better higher education. It is still for elite class who can bear the high fee structure of those self-financing institutions. How will our dream of 'Education for All' come true.

Self-financing institutions have been established with the motto of extension of knowledge. Majority of we Indians are still literates. We need to be educated. Here higher education can be instrumental to educate the society and that knowledge may be utilized for preparing and developing better products both quantitatively and qualitatively Empowerment is required to develop, to grow. It is life, feebleness is death. By extension of knowledge giving vocational and professional training, we may rejuvenate our majority of the population, our people may be empowered by inculcating in them the feeling of entrepreneurship, self-employment and self-help. Still empowerment may be considered with providing them skillful knowledge like IT etc. Proliferation of such education is required and due to limited resources and lackdaisal efforts of our government that has not become possible. Are self-financing institutions reliable means to empower us? Are they really extending the knowledge and that knowledge is really producing new knowledge? Are they reliable means to empower us. Are they really generating self-employment and entrepreneurship?

Are they furthering education and linking it with enriched tradition and culture? Are they moving hand to hand to developed countries in information technology etc. to meet the pace and demand of this hitech age?

These questions must be addressed timely and properly. We may derive inferences from the above discussion that self-financing of higher education can be seen from both the sides. One it is a kind of movement, extending education facilities to the unreached population that is covering the uncovered population. In that sense higher education through self-financing mode has been able to reach to the aspirant class. On the other hand, due to its fee structure (relatively much higher) it could reach or it could extend higher education courses to the limited group, those are comparatively elite capable of affording the higher fees structure. In that sense higher education through self-financing mode has been limited to elite class only. At the same time the establishment of S.F. higher education institutions are still struggling with the qualified trained permanent manpower. As well as many of the institution they lack in proper infrastructural facilities. These shortcomings need proper attention to ensure quality control in self-financed higher education as it is evident from the existing scenario of S.F. higher education. As such institution have been extending higher education where regular institutions could not reach. Realising this fact self-financing higher education institutions need to organise themselves and demand from the concerning authorities to recognize them at par with regular higher education institutions in its all respects.

References

1. Nirmal, P.K., "Education at Doors"
2. Monthly "Kurukshetra".
3. Monthly Journal "Yojana".
4. Report, National Knowledge Commission.

19

Self-Financing *vs.* Relevance

Dr. Veena Singh

Destiny of India is in the hands of 550 million people below the age of 25 who will benefit the most from the new knowledge initiatives. The proportion of our population, in the age of 18–24, that enters the world of higher education is around 7 percent, which is only one-half of the average for Asia. The National Knowledge Commission (NRC) therefore, recommends creation of "1500 universities nationwide, that would enable India to attain a gross enrolment ration of at least 15 percent by 2015."

It has given recommendations regarding reforms in existing public universities, undergraduate colleges, regulatory structure, financing, quality, creation of national universities as centers of academic excellence and access to marginalized and excluded groups.

The universities perform a critical role in the economy and society. Therefore, they must be flexible, innovative and creative. They have to be accountable to the society. The number of universities and colleges have to be increased several times to meet the demands.

In my opinion the opening of self-financing institutions in India should be based on *demand and supply ratio, you get what you pay for and winds of change*. The following datas which has been extracted from recent news-papers will prove my point of view.

Demand and Supply

I have taken examples of health, information and technology sector and teachers in general for formal education.

(i) **Health:** In India, there is on an average one qualified doctor for 1 thousand population. In U.P. the ratio was even worse, here ratio is one for 5,000 population (according to report of health department there are 38,950 allopathic doctors, 0.2 per thousand population—*Dainik Jagran,* 18th September, 2007)

(ii) **IT Sector :** Asia's first Discovery Park to be opened in IIIT Allahabad. Establishment of the park will benefit the students pursuing the research. Institutional Park will have nine centers. It is worth to mention that till date there is only one discovery park in the world i.e., Peridue University. Yet another achievement of IIT i.e., institute will very soon open a network of digital library in ASEAN countries. The budget for the project is estimated between 250 to 300 crores.

Four institutions of the country IIT, IIM, JNU and DU listed among the top 200 educational institutions of the world. IIT was ranked 57th and TIM 68th in the list. (Dainik Jagran, 7th August, 2007). Institutions like Howard, Cambridge and Oxford are in the top rank. This clearly reveals that the progress we have made in IT sectors only in recent years.

IIT is making world's smallest microchip with an aim to promote the micro-engineering. The budget of the project is excepted to around Rs. 200 crore (*Dainik Jagran,* 27th April, 2007)

(iii) **Teachers:** In Allahabad district the teacher-student ratio was 1:76 and 1:64 in 2004-05 and 2005-06 respectively. This ration reflects the condition of education in our country and shows that there is a dearth of qualified teachers which can be overcome by opening of more and more self-financing or Government Teacher's Training Centers.

You Get What Pay for

Wealth comes from knowledge and communication instead of natural resources and physical labour. In eighties when our hon'ble Prime Minister, Sri. Rajeev Gandhi plan to introduce the computers in the country he was looked upon with scepticism. It was the result of his speculation that this year four students from IIM were offered a package of 1 crore per annum and many students were offered package of several lakhs per year. This shows that it is worth paying a tution fee of Rs. 10 lakh per annum in IIT's and IIM's because the candidate is going to get back the money spent in 4 years within a year or so.

In USA some private colleges are very expensive. To receive excellent service and job the students attained first two years at a community colleges with lower cost and easier admission policies and then get themselves admitted in premier institutions for remaining two years. This reduces cost of education and student can get value of their money spent.

Winds of Change

Higher education at a distance has significantly contributed to Indian National Development on various counts including community development, nationwide training program for the workforce and empowerment of women etc. To day there are 11 open universities, 106 dual mode universities distance education centers! institutions in the country accommodating more than 2.8 million, 429 academic programs and 3,817 courses through network of 105 regional centers, 4,229 study centers and 62,000 tutors or counselors.

In recently opened Rajarshi Open University, Allahabad for B.Ed. admission more than 10,000 candidates appeared in entrance test and the seats were only 500 (23rd August, 2007, *Dainik Jagran*) i.e. only 5 percent of the students are going to get admission. The datas shows that there is much more scope of opening of teachers training institutions in our country which is possible only by privatization and self-financing of higher education.

Summary and Suggestions

There will be 10 lakhs new jobs in coming 5 years and we will not be able to fulfill it by trained professionals.

Merits:

It is therefore concluded that there is urgent need of

new higher education institutions like medical colleges, IIT's IIM's and teacher training institutions to cope up the demands. As we are aware higher education in any form is not on priority list of Government. So if we really want to strengthen these sectors, then the only way is the privatization and self-financing. By producing quality persons in these sectors in present era of globalization we will be able to compete in international scene also.

Demerits:

1. In my opinion strict quality control and fulfillment of norms laid down by different governing bodies must be followed.
2. Another caution is that we have to check commercialization of higher education. It can be achieved by quality control etc., which I have already dealt

Remedial Steps

Government is aware of problems of commercialization and sub-standard teaching. Keeping this problem in mind a meeting of ail VCs of various universities have planned to organize national seminar in the coming October, 2007 with an aim to improve higher education in the examination, changes in fee structure, to connect all universities and colleges (367 universities and 18,000 colleges) of the country to ICT and facilities of virtual classrooms, tele-video conferencing and digital library.

(Newspaper, *India Today,* People's Democracy, Vol. X February, 2006, NKC Report 2006, Vijender Sharma)

20

Self-Financing in Higher Education Prospects and Retrospects: Its Relevance, Effectively and Empowerment

Sanjay Kumar
Dr. C.B. Pathak

Education is considered as an investment both at the individual level and society level, but the benefits from such investments are not immediate and quick. All levels of education require adequate investment to be made by the society though the degree of investment varies from one level to another. Primary education by nature requires lower investment per pupil but in aggregate the investment will be very high as primary education is mandatory in most of the developing and under developed countries. Secondary education level relatively requires more investment individual-wise than the primary education by nature demands higher investment both individually and collectively.

Prospects and Retrospects of Self-Financing in Higher Education

The financing of higher education system in India presents a big paradise. With the liberalization of the economy in the early 1990s and increasing dropout levels at privacy and secondary education levels, the investment in higher education has taken a reverse gear. Rather than accelerating investment levels in higher education sector to prepare individuals with high caliber and qualification, the state is slowly limiting its role learning its media core institution to fend for themselves.

Higher education in India is in the financial stress. Higher education in India is characterized by massive public investment, though the investment in still regarded as much below optimum demand for higher educated manpower will increase, substantially in the near future and this will impel central focus on the quality and quantity of human resource produced by the higher education system. To achieve this system requires large additional resources. Increasing needs stemming from population growth, need for modernization and the limited nature of resources are problems facing financing of education.

India is way behind other developing countries not to say about any comparison with the developed countries. The public expenditure on education is only about 3 percent of the Gross National Product (GNP). More particularly, only 0.301 percent of GDP is spent on higher education in India and this has been falling in recent years.

Table 20.1 : Growth of Higher Education Institutions and Enrolment in India

Year	*Universities*	*Colleges*	*Total HEIs*	*Enrolment (in million)*
1947-48	20	496	516	0.2
1950-51	28	578	606	0.2
1960-61	45	1,819	1,864	0.6
1970-71	93	3,277	3,370	2.0
1980-81	123	4,738	4,861	2.8
1990-9 1	184	5,748	5,932	4.4
2000-01	266	11,146	11,412	8.8
2005-06	348	17,625	17,973	10.5

HEI = Higher Education Institution.

According to analysis of a committee, the recurring expenditure on education in the year 2015 would be Rs. 1,80,000 crore. The capital expenditure would be Rs. 88,900 crore spend over the next 15 years. This is based on population projections to the year 2015 and working on the basis that the goals of an education policy would be to universalize education in the age group 5–14 achieve a 75 percent enrolment rate in higher secondary (age group 15–19) and a 20 percent enrolment in colleges and professional education (age group 20-24).

The projected expenditure on education to meet the mentioned goals works out to these times the current expenditure. The government's share would amount to Rs. 1,17,099 crore. At a projected growth rate of eight per cent GDP, the total education expenditure would be 3.15 percent of the GNP. The total population that would have achieved testing population will be about 5.6 percent and 9.8 percent depending on a GDP growth rate of 6 percent or 10 percent per year respectively. The total number of teachers in all sectors would have to more than double frame the existing 49.25 lakhs to a range of 93.47 lakhs to 119.15 lakhs.

Although privatization of education is not a new malady, it has been in existence from times immemorial but not in its present form, as a commercial venture. The ancient Gurukuls were private academies run by our learned seers and sages, which sometimes enjoyed royal patronage in the form of jagirs being gifted to fund their upkeep, yet they were free from any state control. Later with the advent of Buddhism, education became an organized activity being provided in Maths and Vihars, enjoying patronage of the ruling elite. An institution of an all India character which came into existence without reference to government grants was the Vishwabharti, which was founded and endowed by Gurudev Rabindranath Tagore (Naik and Nurullah, 1974). Tagore set-up an ashram school at Bolpur, called Shantiniketan and an international university known as Vishvabharti. At last tired by there constant begging expenditions as Mahatma Gandhi called them and due to his failing health, Gurudev appealed to Gandhi to assume trusteeship and arrange funds to sustain this national asset (Bhattacharya, 2001). Thus as a consequence of Mahatma Gandhi's appeal to his countrymen's philanthropy and the donations given by the Birla brothers, this truly internationals institution got a new lease of life in 1937 (Bhattacharya, 2001).

Yet another outstanding example of establishing single handedly a national university in the holy city of Varanasi needs mention. Mahatma Gandhi, Pt. Madan Mohan Malviya, the 'Princely beggar' as Mahatma Gandhi called him set out to collect funds and single handedly established the Banaras Hindu University. This institution later went on to receive government grants and has become a central university today.

The Jamia Millia Islamia was a true national university which declined government recognition because its promoters preferred, "the hardship and or deals of an honorable independence to the enervrating security of a permanent grant which would Frustate its noblest ambitions. The Jamia had no permanent fund but its biggest, source of income was the large number of its supporters called 'Hamdardane Jamia', who contributed part of their earnings to support Jamia (Naik and Murulah, 1974).

The Gurukul University is another example of a self-financing nationalist educational institution which refused government grants from its very inception and therefore remained free from government interference and committed to its aim of revival of ancient Indian ideals.

In 1937, Mahatma Gandhi came out with the 'Wardha Scheme' of basic education which was to be self-supporting, self-financing scheme of education. Sustaining it self on the resource raised by the sale of the craft related produce, made by the students themselves.

Privately established and funded schools were initially set-up by missionaries of all religious beliefs and hues, but in recent years with the concept of self-financing education changing rapidly, many private players have set-up schools as commercial ventures. Dr. T.M.A. Pai, a visionary, and pioneer in self-financing professional education, established the 'Manipal Medical College' which was fully financed, managed and controlled by a private trust and sustained by the fee collected from the students.

This model institution expand its horizons into other professional fields and also acted as a catalyst for privately funded professional colleges. Some of these privately managed and financed colleges, have earned a reputation for themselves by providing better infrastuctuval facilities, faculty and teaching than many resource starved, publicly funded professional colleges in the country.

Relevance Effectivity and Empowerment of Self-Financing in Higher Education

Only 6-7 percent of the target population of 18-23 years old as against 50-51 percent of students getting university education in OECD countries (Manjula, 2004). With the control and state governments unable to allocate more funds, a financial crises is looming large in the higher education the escalating costs of the system and the dwindling resources has initiated a shift in policy towards privatization.

A shift in thinking from reliance on public funds to privatization or private funding of education is a recent phenomenon. The concept itself has undergone a change. The Gandhian concept of self-supporting, publicly controlled enterprise education is now regarded as 'self-financing private enterprise'.

All the above measures are aimed at raising the financial status of higher education institutions by raising their resources so that dependence on States and Central Governments is reduced and self-sufficiency increased.

This would unable institutions to develop adequate infrastructure to improve access, quality and equity, which are the major concerns in funding of higher education.

The declining support for higher education from governments and endowment has necessiated institution to start self-financing courses to supplement the traditional sources of income. It is imperative that there self-financing courses be demand and performance driver.

The international commission on education for the 21st century in its report entitled. Learning : The Treasurs within (1996) suggested that: "It is not only justifiable but also desirable to raise money from private sources in order to ease pressure on national-budgets."

The Pinnayya Committee report on UGC funding of institution of higher education also encouraged universities to raise resources themselves but restrained the UGC to cut down on block grants as a result of extra fund raised.

It was also suggested that Universities must forge a partnership within industry. It must offer consultancy and research opportunities in return for access to latest technology and improved employment prospects for student through summer projects and internship programs.

Mushroom Growth of Higher Educational Institution and Quality Control

The resultant outcome of self-financing in higher education has been the establishment of colleges, which are founded, funded and run by private agencies with the sole aim of earning product. This trend has adversely affected the system of higher education in terms of equity considerations because admissions to these courses are based on the principle of ability to pay rather than on merit. Also they are linked to students and parents need rather than societal needs.

This is view of above fact that is, the mushrooming of higher educational institutes has generated growing concerns for the quality of higher education. In order that institutions do not slide back into mediocrity, there is a need to keep a watch on their functioning to view them critically both from inside and outside (S.A., Kareem, 1999).

It is necessary to develop effective quality assurance and assessment systems that are internationality standardized (Green and Harvey, 1993).

The concern about quality of education and quality assurance through a suitable external mechanism is evident from the fact that more than 180 national quality assurance agencies in about 100 countries have been established in the past decade on so.

In India, the quality assessment agencies are the National Assessment and Acceditation Council (NAAC), established by UGC and the National Board of Accreditation (NBA), under the All India Council for Technical Education (AICTE).

NAAC's impact has been felt by institutions in all aspects of their functioning pedagogical, managerial and administrative. Institutions took up initiatives beyond the mandatory requirement of the affiliating system. Management often able to introduce major changes on the grounds that it would demonstrate a commitment to quality (Antony, S., 2002).

References

1. Antony, S. (2002). Institutional Acceratitation in India. *International Higher Education, Spring.*
2. Bhattarcharya, Sabyasachi (ed.).(2001). *The Mahatma and the Poet.* New Delhi: National Trust.
3. Green, D. and Harvey, L. (1993). Quality Assurance in Western Europe Trends, Practices and Issues. Santa, T.W., Anderson, C.L. Borendt, B. (Editors). *Proceedings, Fifth International Conference on Assessing quality in Higher Education, Indian University. Purdure University, Indian Polis.*
4. Kareem, S.A. (1999). Is Accreditation an answer to quality assurance? *University News,* 37 (35).
5. Naik, J.P. and Narullah, Syed. (1974). *A Students History of Education in India,* 1800-1973. Delhi, The Macmillan Co. of India.

21

Privatization of Education *vs.* Commercialization

Km Jyoti Gupta

Introduction

The impact of education is intense and pervasive on almost all human activities. In the knowledge economy. Professional and personal development of people through education and training are critical for ensuring social progress and economic growth. In economic sense, investment in education is profitable. The socio-economic benefits reaped by students over the entire span of working life are, therefore, accepted axiomatically.

Privatization and Commercialization

It is generally perceived that the costs of not acquiring new knowledge and skills are more than the costs of obtaining them. In fact, the costs of provision of educational services borne by the government or private providers and students/parents, are therefore, considered equal to or less than the expenditure incurred by the beneficiary students. The expected gains from education and training generate high demand for educational services, which when not provided by the government or other philanthropic organizations, encourage private investors and entrepreneurs to offer various courses on self-financing basis.

Privatization of higher education is based on the assumption that it will inhance the efficiency of the system when the government buys academic services from producers or subsidises students to buy them. Further, to the extent that the private sector takes up the responsibility of providing education, the government will be relieved of its burden. It has also been claimed that education, particularly higher education, enhance the earning capabilities of the students and, therefore, the burden of financing should largely be shared by the beneficiaries.

While there is some merit in involving private bodies in the financing and management of higher education. Complete privatization might not be in the best interests of education. It will lead to a skewed development of education. In that only market oriented courses will be introduced particularly at the higher education stage. Further basic research will suffer. Privatization may also to lead to commercialization of education.

When profit motives dominate and quality of education is sacrificed or fee and other charges levied in excess of expenditure on service provided such educational ventures are generally termed as commercial. A major consequence corn be the inability of the poor and the underprivileged sections to get the benefits of education which for them can be the principal means for upward economic and social mobility.

Commercialization of Higher Education

It is observed that commercialization in education is associated with the institutions. Which are under private management. Because most such institutions claim to operate on no-profit and no-loss basis, the extent of revenue generation for profit motives is difficult to determine due to financial and accounting gimmicks as practiced by them.

In the wake of liberalization policies, a large number of technical and professional institution have been allowed to be established by apex bodies like UGC, AICTE and other professional statuary bodies, on self-financing basis. The activities of most of these institutions are not necessarily philanthropic. The self-financing institutions are sponsored by the trusts, which are often supported by industrial houses and commercial organizations.

Tax laws are favorable to educational institutions since donors enjoy tax concessions to the extent of 50-125 percent for donations to different educational and research activities. As per the directive of the Supreme Court of India, they adopt wide ranging high fee policies for free and payment seats and management quota and foreign students. The institutions hardly provide any information on fees that they charge nor do they keep proper records so as to evade and avoid legal actions. Such on act of fund raising is not only unethical but also tantamount to commercialization of education. And the wide spread increase in such activities is attributable mainly to inadequate government support for creation of facilities to meet the growing demand for quality education. Lack of effective control and regulation by apex bodies aggravate the problems of commercialization in education.

Some institutions operating on commercial basis exploit the motivated students without assuring quality of education and, in effect, have brought down quality of education. Commercial shops, having freedom to close any time, have left the students half way in the process of learing. And the institution that survive such competitions excessively exploit students by way of levying un-economic fees and charges for various services.

Present Status of Commercialization in India

In India 40 percent of the total population do not have worthwhile assets for generation of income to support their minimum requirements for maintaining a decent standard of living. In views of this, commercialization of education has hardly offered any opportunity of learning to them, and this is the reason that they have lagged for behind insofor as their contribution to productivity growth and economic development is concerned.

In general, commercialization of education is not accepted and approved by the society, particularly by the countries like India. Moreover, India's long history, tradition and culture of imparting knowledge and training have put pious obligations on the duty conscious society for providing worthwhile education.

Suggestions

1. The functioning of public and private sector partnership requires to be reviewed for effective management of education systems.
2. The Government particularly educational councils should evolve acceptable norms for effective functioning and monitoring of institutions.
3. The fees and other charges should be levied in relation to the costs of education.
4. The institutions, moreover, should regularly file their Income Tax Returns to ensure transparency in financial management.

References

1. Ambani-Birla Report, 2000.
2. Ansari, M.M.; Commercialisation of Education Encyclopaedia of Indian Education Vol. I, p. 309.
3. Azad, J.L., *Educational Financing Encyclopaedia,* Vol.1, p. 558.
4. Mukarjee, Kamal Kishore, Social Thought, Vivek Prakashan Jawahar Nagar, Delhi-7, p. 526.
5. Mukharjee, Radha Kamal, *A General Theory of Society,* p. 22.
6. News paper, *Amar Ujala,* A Report on Higher Education, Kanpur 18 Sept., 2007.
7. Prasad, Kamal Kishore, Commercialization of Higher Education, *Pratiyogita Darpan,* July, 2001, p. 2258.
8. Verma, Aneesh Kumar, Problem of Educational values in the Era of globalization, Newspaper, *Dainik Varanasi,* Thursday 19th Oct., 2006, p. 8.

22

Challenges and Responses of Higher Education in India

Mrs. Prem Prabha Singh

Globally the contemporary higher education system in faced with an unprecedented challenge, precisely because of dramatic change brought about by metamorphasing economic and political realistic of the contemporary world. Higher education as the Apex of the educational hierarchy / structure deserves our care and attention both for its quantitative and qualitative improvement. It is essential for human resource development in general and education of all types in particular educational reform generally begins with the issue whether education is a 'public good' and should we try to keep it outside the commercial realm if we can do it at all ? The 'public good' either is linked to socio-democratic ideals of equality of opportunity, access for many, and ultimately also quality. The contention that the availability of the higher education should not be limited by financial considerations also appears to be valid especially in a developing country such as India where the largest section of the population comprises lower middle and lower income groups without much of economic and social security. It the light of the fact that even though a higher education does not automatically guarantee a higher paying job or greater income. The importance of higher education can further be seen in the context of its inter-generational impart. In fact a college/ university is increase a prerequisite for opportunities for effective labor force participation and for economic and social mobility.

Higher education has entered a period of significant change as educational institutions attempt to respond to the challenges, opportunities and responsibilities facing them in the new century. In the rapidly changing circumstances, they are no longer only the knowledge producers or vital human capital formation instruments but are also important service provides as well.

The expectations of student and parents have changed. Considerably, they are also aware of the need to acquire even more sophisticated professional skills to equip themselves for a complex labour market.

Current Status

A majority of the colleges, being arts, science and commerce colleges after education in humanities, natural science, arts and commerce. There are about 550 engineering and technical colleges, 655 medical colleges, nearly 600 management institutions, 700 teacher education training colleges and 1100 polytechnics about the fourth of the total number of colleges are private colleges of two types privately managed but publicly funded known as (government) unaided college. The number of women's colleges has recorded as substantial increase. In 2001-02, India has 1500 women's colleges with enrolment of women standing at 37.659 of the total student enrollment. However, Girls in general, have shown more inclination towards non-professional stream as

22.1: Growth in Higher Education in India

Institutions	*1950-51*	*1990-91*	*1996-97*	*2001-02*
University	30	117	214	248
Colleges	750	7346	9703	12342
Enrolment	263	4925	6755	8000
Teachers	24	2727	321	396

Source : UGC Annual Reports, 2001-2002.

is evident from the fact that 87 percent of the enrolment in this category is in arts, science and commerce while only 13% of the total girl student have made their way to the professional courses.

The higher education system in India encompasses a vastly heterogeneous students body demographically diverse (age, gender, region, social background, etc.) educationally disadvantage (most of them without the traditional qualification for entering into higher education and who have had no other opportunities to make up for the lost time) and economically weak (large may arity belonging to low and lower middle encomia groups). Graduate education in India is fairly competition, especially the quality business management, science and technology education, leading to the entry of a few in the premier institutions of the country for the rest the choice is extremely limited as they have to pay same or higher level of fee in private institutions must of which are not realty known for imparting and maintaining quality education.

As part of its responsibility to enhance the quality of the university/college teachers, the scheme of academic staff college was launched by University Grants Commission (UGC) in 1986 - 87, under which 45 such colleges have been set-up so far. These colleges conduct four week orientation program for training new teachers with innovative techniques and also 3–4 week orientation programs for training new teachers with innovative techniques and also 3–4 week refresher course in various disciplines for in service teachers to enable them to update their knowledge similarly in order to discharge its responsibility towards the maintenance and promotion of standards of education. The University Grants Commissions (UGC) in 1994 established the National Assessment and Accreditation Council (NAAC) for accreditation of the educational institutions as part of its strategy towards quality assurance in higher education. The current educational Media Production Centre are state-of-the art technological facilities that significantly enrich the learning packages in the realm of higher education. satellite based teleconferencing networks is being developed on an experimental basis in co-operation with the India Space

Research Organization (ISRO) for providing interactive teaching-learning support a distance education programs offered by open universities in India.

Although various monitoring agencies such as UGO and AICTE have been making substantive efforts in order to update the higher education system.

The Forces Dreaming Change in Higher Education Today

Knowledge explosion, globalisations, accelerating technological change. Now, linear knowledge transfer, age of knowledge, changing societal needs, financial imperatives technology drivers and market forces. All these factors have led to a paradigm shift away in the education system which means more towards learning rather than instructions, which is technology—intensive rather than manpower.

Suggestions

1. UGC and other agencies must ensure with respect to each institution the quality assurance, the provision of public information to all stakeholders.
2. The quality of training for teachers and the quality of teaching in higher education institutions demand top priority.
3. Universities should be capable of providing academic and administrative leadership within a decentralized system of administrations. This would require complete end to the political appointments.
4. The funding bodies should make such a review a condition of public funding. The allocation of funds have to be balanced with the students growing expectations for technology support and services.
5. More support and encouragement are particularly required in case of those students from families with income in adequate to support higher studies of their children. Special provisions are made for such disadvantaged groups in public funded institutions.
6. Institutions need to review their programs to consider, whether such programs have the right balance of breadth and depth areas of studies and

professional shall such as communication, self-management and planning.

7. University should build international links to enrich and increase effectiveness, *e.g.*, IIM Ahmedabad, Banglore, Kolkata have established student exchange programs.
8. Teaching Assistantship to the PG students for conducting tender graduate classes and tutorials must become a common practice (earning while learning). The university system also has a great responsibility to the society as a whole constructing towards generating awareness and assisting adult literacy, population control, village uplift, environmental awareness etc. through NSS.

Conclusion

Since Indian higher education system is considered to be highly credible, especially among third world countries. This is the appropriate time to change and attract, at least the third world students, to whom India could be projected to be offering world class education at affordable cost. Any loss of theme would cause irreversible damage in terms of loss of market, credibility, resources and opportunity to transform to meet the new challenges. India at present is in unique position to emerge as leading educationist in Asia, Africa and in many Islands under-developed countries). Which in turn help our employment problems of educated youth who are in abundence. Hence, the crying need of the hour is to unite, plan, work togather with almost sincerity to achieve the aforesaid goal.

References

1. Hanumanthappa, K. (1993): *Challenges and Responses and Higher Education in India : Relevance of Sri Sathiya Sai Systems of Education,* University News, November 8.
2. Mohanty Jagnath (2003): *Current Trends in Higher Education,* Deep Publications, New Delhi.
3. Narkhede Sameer Pralhad (2001) : *Challenges of Higher Education in India:* Puls, Sarup & Sons. New Delhi.

23

Self-Finance Institutions: A New Imperialism

Avis Chintamani

To meet the challenges of 21st century and to acquire a competitive edge, the higher education system has to transform to make it more socially relevant, information and technology oriented, diversified and of high quality. Our country has accepted this goal of modernization with the purpose of marching together with progressive counties of the world. Infact, modernization is a concept symbolizing a movement of progressive thinking, evolution of better and better techniques of production and scientific advancement with the main objectives of removing blind beliefs, destructive attitudes and worthless society, we see that progressive and developed nations of the world are marching ahead from 'State Controlled' to an 'an educational system driven by market force' from 'teacher centerd' to 'learner centred' education. These changes make new demands and pose fresh changes to our established education systems and practices and therefore, a time has come when we have to reappraise their role and functions, the present administrative structure finances of university management. The state with its slow moving machinery alone is unable to produce the genius of Indian people and thus giving rise to the participation of private sector. In these days of globalization people cannot be blamed for wanting better education for their children. Very few central and state universities offer courses by which students can earn a decent living.

There is no argument that the basic responsibility of any developing country should be towards better primary and secondary education since both are important for students to proceed towards better higher education because higher education is very important for economic development and over all national growth. Higher education has to become internationally competitive. It would be detrimental for the government to listen the World Bank that the development of higher education should follow the market principle. For this purpose liberalization and privatization become important.

For this purpose UGC has to go in favour of greater autonomy for universities through in a given academic frame. Infact, the academic council should formulate a strategy for this and empower colleges within the given norms to confer a degree that gives students more credibility in the profession on choice. And talking about universities and colleges, they would also have more freedom to bring and carry out innovation in whatever area they choose without any worry. It is purely true that many of the great universities Howard, Oxford, Cambridge grew because they were independent and even our own great modern universities such as Banaras, Allahabad and Calcutta had their glory days when they were considerably more self-financing than they currently are.

To have effective autonomy in the long run UGC has to involve itself to have a considerable hold on the colleges and universities. In this context, the UGC has set-up a National Assessment and Accreditation Council (NAAC), an independent organization to assess and accredit colleges and universities. It has developed an instrument and methodology to judge quality in totality in educational institutions. This way many universities have gone through this process and many colleges are being assessed. But as far as accrediting colleges and ranking them by an accreditation or ranking body is concerned, there is nothing so special or new in it. Students, parents and teachers already know which college or university is good for which course or which facilities they offer. By introducing ranking and accreditation these facts will become more official than they are now. Then the best teachers would get hired for students and value based education will be imparted to the students. Colleges with better educational facilities or better structured courses will obviously have a better result than the others. Since there exists uniformity in the course structures and academic facilities in most of the colleges, one can actually differentiate between them on the basis of their results and judge their true academic standard.

But if we go deep study of National Education Policy 1986, up dated in 1992 and its implementation. The proposal made for the total privatization of higher education from undergraduate to postgraduate deserves a close look.

The biggest giant standing in the path of progress is corruption. Those with high political connections are allowed and will be allowed to open institutions resulting in the mushrooming of what, are called 'Self-financing institutions'. The formation of the governing management of the private institutions and universities merits critical examination. Private management will not be under the control either of the government or of the UGC. The sponsoring committee of private universities will have the power to appoint the vice-chancellors and the members of the Board of Governors and only one representative from the government will add a feather to it. There will be no senate and no elected representatives. This undemocratic formation of management is highly detrimental to the interest of higher education. If compared to democratic governance structure, we will find it is always in favour of growth promotion and extension of a quality academic environment and will be acting as a safety value for the student community. Private management will start their educational institutions with purely commercial motives. Most of them do not want to invest any substantial amount in infrastructure development. Many universities and colleges under the governance of private management will not follow the norms and regulations framed by the UGC in respect of student admissions and procedures on curriculum, evaluation process and appointment qualification. The rigid regulations on practical training and field work important for professional courses will not be obeyed. Under these circumstances, substandard instead of quality education will be the ultimate harvest that the students will have to reap. Education will be treated as a marketable commodity and degrees and diplomas can be purchased at a premium without going through the regular educational process.

There will also be a decline in the appointment of teaching staff. The private institutions may flout the prescribed norms of UGC and can select candidates of poorer merit or extraneous conditions such as payment of donations, bribery and gifts to influential persons. Moreover, the private management may not pay salaries according to the UGC scale and admissible allowances though teachers will be forced to sign to the effect that they are being paid in full. To make huge profits, there will be a hike in fees which will go beyond the reach of the common man. Taking the economic conditions into account, we may safely conclude that most people will be deprived of higher education if the government is bent on cutting subsidies ending the "grant-in-aid system" and allowing educational institution to raise their own fund. It is true a new imperialism in the form of higher education will gradually overtake the educational sphere.

Suggestions

1. Though many universities and colleges have objected to National Assessment and Accreditation Council but commission must ensure that the institutions of higher learning should follow the objectives of continuous improvement in the quality of education. The government and UGC should honestly and sincerely implement the policies and there should be transparency in it.
2. More emphasis should be given on the improvement of the quality of teachers and to keep a check on the salaries and other emoluments paid to the teachers. They must be according to the norms of UGC.
3. There should be a healthy relation between higher education and economic development. India has to produce man power who not only can earn a decent

loving but can march together with the progressive countries of the world by adding more and more to national income of the country.

4. Necessary control and monitoring mechanism must be developed to ensure quality education at reasonable cost. Management may not close or wind up any course at any time when they find it to be less profitable and may force students to take up courses against their will with the sole objective of collecting higher fees.

24

Privatization of Higher Education in India

Dr. Neelam Singh

In India, over the years, there have been private initiatives in education initially for philanthropic reasons and eventually in professional and even in general higher education not only to meet the growing demands but also to realize the huge and quick profits potential. Privatization of higher education has emerged in several forms and types in the recent decade in India. One, privatisation within government higher education institutions take place in the form of introducing self-financing courses with government institutions; two converting government aided private institutions into private self-financing institutions; three, allowing to expand self-financing private institutions with recognition and also without recognition. The objectives of higher education and basic research for any society, particularly one striving to grow into a knowledge society, are not only to address the knowledge needs of present time, but also to project the knowledge needs of the future, as far as possible. It is the responsibility of the state to try to determine the futuristic vision with appropriate funding.

Commercial private higher education emerges from market forces and tied to economic and global forces. They thrive on the principles of commercialism, primary focus on vocàtional courses and highly pragmatic. Their commercial thrust is training jobs, indeed, part of the curriculum is industrial training. Commercializaton of higher education can have adverse implication both in terms of equity and access. Comodification of education will not serve the long range interest of nation. It could lead to truncated growth and top sided development of higher education. Distance education is yet another area where potential of commercialization are quite high. Narrow focus is its strength as well weakness. It is a strength as long as there is demand for such specific nature of the courses and a weakness once such a demand is satiated. Moreover, the built-in set-up/ infrastructure do not allow them to diversify. They cater to the unmet demands or rather demand-absorbing from the nonuniversity higher education sector.

Ownership of these private institutions ranges between a spectrum of substantially weaker and stronger commercial institutions. Indeed, there are chain of institutions from Kindergarden to higher levels of education by well-known business groups and corporate sector. Since 1993 with the Supreme Court judgment, growth of commercial higher education in the name of capitation fee or self-financing colleges is mushrooming. The private institutions include colleges, training centers, etc. Neither the Department of Education nor the University Grants Commission collect, compile and publish the information on the size and growth of institutions and enrolments on this rapidly growing private higher education.

There are also different types of these private institutions— May of the self-financing engineering colleges and management institutions are affiliated to the conventional universities (examples as found in Tamil Nadu, Karnataka and Andhra Pradesh). In which, the course structure, design, curriculum and the pattern of examination fall within the purview of the national or state pattern. On the other side, several of these self-financing private institutions are also non-affiliating to any universities and cater to the demand of the corporate sector nationally and internationally. Whether the private institutions follow multi-faculty or discipline are decided by the individual institutions.

Since the program and courses are make driven and each private institution decides on their own the course and subjects it offers. Hence, they also have a free hand to introduce new programs and discard the old.

Student is the power while faculty is weak in these private institutions. Indeed, the faculty lack the position, power and autonomy as they traditionally enjoy at universities. Basically they serve to students and their practical orientations in commercial private institutions. These institutions rely on part time faculty and may be drawn from full time faculty at public universities (and hence do not add to further employment opportunities). When employing full time faculty, they pay meager salary. Perhaps many of them have neither practical nor academic expertise and lack training these institutions make huge profits, sometimes recover more than their recurring costs (full of recurring cost plus part of the capital cost). Such institutions survive as long as there is a demand for their services and the students are willing to pay for such job directed training.

The Government of India in its Prime Minister's Council on Trade and Industry, appointed a committee to suggest required reforms in the education sector, along with other sectors (headed by M. Ambani and K. Birla). It strongly suggested for full cost recovery (user pays principle) from students even in public higher education institutions through hike in fees and introduction of self-financing courses and seats; shifting of resources from higher to primary level of education that government should leave higher education altogether to the private sector and confine itself to elementary and secondary education. Further, the report urged the private university bill to be passed and also suggested that the user pays principle be strictly enforced in higher education, supplemented by loans and grants to economically and socially backward sections of society. (Ambani-Birla, 2001)

In developing countries like India, it is only be profit, which thrives these institutions and efficiency is jeopardized, the important dimensions of complementarily and competitions found in the U.S. private higher education sector boosts the growth and survival of both the public and private higher institutions, which is conspicuously absent in India.

There are a number of important factors that led to emergence and rapid expansion of private higher education in India. They are classified here as the conventional pull and push factors. In addition to these, the external factors that have been conducive for the growth of private higher education is also discussed.

All over the world including India, there has been rapid expansion and demand for higher education known as massification of higher education. The conventional university sector is not able to cater to the demands of the new sections of the rapidly growing eligible age group population for higher education. As an alternative, private enterprises are sought to accommodate this evolving pressure on higher education in various forms, types and levels.

Conventional university course are not able to cater to the immediate demands of the market as it takes considerable amount of time for a change within the formal higher education/university system. This academic inflexibility boosted the rapid development of private initiatives in higher education. Perhaps, many providers/stakeholders in many of these private institutions are the one who struggled to change the formal system to suit to the needs of the students who, in turn, demand depending upon the marketability of a course, the emphasis being pragmatism.

The conventional institutions lack the responsiveness of higher education to labor market demands implying business participation in governing boards of institutions, the creation of financial incentives for joint industry university research, corporate sponsored internships for students and part time academic appointments for professionals from the productive sector. Alternatively such a nexus between academics and industry is met by private institutions with multi-disciplinary and/or inter disciplinary course, which are short-term in nature with a very narrow focus. Hence, led to proliferation of short term/market oriented courses. However, leaving a few reputed private higher learning institutions, majority of them are education shops catering to the majority of the students, who are willing to pay with a desperate hope to get into the job market.

In short, these private institutions marketed their service in technology courses varying from hi-tech to fashion technology; management courses ranging from institutional management to hotel management and promised to produce not only employable youth but also to place them in jobs. Expenditure compression referred as resource constraint of the government on account of economic reforms led to financial privatization of higher education in various forms such as reduced allocation to higher education.

"Education is not the filling of a bucket, but the lightining of a fire." –*W.B. Yeats*

"The objectives of education is to prepare the young to educate themselves throughout their lives."

–*Robert Maynard Hutchins*

References

1. AICTE (1994), *Report of the High Power Committee for Mobilization of Additional Resources for Technical Education,* All India Council for Technical Education, New Delhi.
2. Ambani, M. and Birla K. (2001), *Report on a Policy Framework for Reforms in Education,* Government of India, New Delhi.
3. Government of India (1992), *Programme of Action on the National Education Policy,* Ministry of Human Resource Development, New Delhi.
4. Government of India (1997), *Approach Paper to the Ninth Five Year Plan, 1997–2002,* Planning Commission, New Delhi.
5. Government of India (1997-2002), *Ninth Five Year Plan : 1997–2002,* Planning Commission, New Delhi.
6. Government of India (2000), *Midterm Appraisal of Ninth Five Year Plan: 1997–2002,* Planning Commission, New Delhi.
7. Government of India (2001), *Approach Paper to the Tenth Five Year Plan, 2002–2007*, Planning Commission, New Delhi.
8. Government of India (2002-2007), *Tenth Five Year Plan : 2002–2007,* Planning Commission, New Delhi.
9. Rani, Geetha P. (2003), "Financing Education in India in the Economic Reform Period Focus on Intra-sectoral Allocation of Resources to Education", in *Globalisation and Challenges of Education,* (ed), NIEPA, 2003.

25

Teaching Motivation of Student-Teachers Studying in Self-Financed Course

Dr. Pratik Upadhyaya
Ruchi Dubey

Today in India, the government and the private sector are providing education. The universities run self-financed courses because of the social requirement of specialized courses and to earn money to meet the growing fund requirements. To meet the growing demand of increasing number of students aspiring to do B.Ed., various self-financed B.Ed., programs are being run in India to provide training to future teachers.

The teachers' knowledge along with their feelings become integrated with the students scheme. When the teacher loves his profession, the students learn to love education.

Teacher's motivation for teaching is a very crucial input in education. In the process of teaching, formulation of learning ends and selection of means is influenced by the level of motivation of the teacher. Kelley et, al. (2000) reported that knowledge of teacher and skills related to instruction is an important factor of teachers' motivation. Mittal (1989) found that teachers who perceived less psychological hindrance and more humanised thrust are more work motivated. Goal orientation is instrumental for long-term teachers' motivation. Teaching motivation among teachers is very important for their success and job satisfaction. When the teacher remains motivated, the students are also motivated towards learning. So, every possible efforts needs to be made to increase the teaching motivation among both male and female student-teachers during the teacher training program because student-teachers with high teaching motivation have found to be more emotionally intelligent, moralistic and controlled and can handle adolescents in a better way (Upadhyaya, 2006).

The present study has been conducted to study the teaching motivation of student teachers studying through self-financed and non-self-financed program.

Objectives: The objectives of the study were:

1. To compare the teaching motivation of student-teachers of self-financed and non-self-financed programs.
2. To compare the teaching motivation of student-teachers of arts stream of self-financed and non-self-financed program.
3. To compare the teaching motivation of student-teachers of science stream of self-financed and non-self-financed program.

Hypotheses : The following hypotheses were formulated and tested :

1. There is no significant difference in teaching motivation of student-teachers of self-financed and non-self-financed program.
2. There is no significant difference in teaching motivation of student-teachers of arts stream of self-financed and non-self-financed program.
3. There is no significant difference in teaching motivation of student-teachers of science stream of self-financed and non-self-financed program.

Methodology: The sample comprises of 164 student-teachers of Allahabad city. Out of which 80 student-teacher belong to self-financed course and 84 belong to non-self-financed course. Teaching Motivation Inventory developed by Pratik Upadhyaya was used to measure teaching motivation. It consisted of 38 items. Out of which 25 statements were positive and 13 were negative. It is a five-point scale.

To analyse the data t-ratio were calculated.

Result and Discussion

Table-25.1 : Mean, S.D. and T-ratio Showing the Difference in Teaching motivation of Student-teachers of Self-financed and Non-self-financed Program.

Programme	*N*	*M*	*S.D.*	*t-ratio*
Self-financed	80	164	13.95	2.67*
Non-self-financed	84	158.43	12.73	

* Significant at .01 level.

Table-24.1 shows that mean teaching motivation scores for student-teachers of self-financed and non-self-financed programs are 164 and 158.43 respectively. It also shows that the value of t-ratio (= 2.67) is significant at .01 level. It means that student-teachers of self-financed and non-self-financed program differ from each other in their teaching motivation. Student-teachers of self-financed program have more teaching motivation in comparison to student-teachers of non-self-financed programme.

Table-25.2 : Mean, S.D. and T-ratio Showing the Difference in Teaching Motivation of Student-teachers of Arts Stream of Self-financed and Non-self-financed Program.

Programme	*N*	*M*	*S.D.*	*t-ratio*
Self-financed	50	163.1	15.495	2.05*
Non-self-financed	58	157.43	12.85	

* Significant at .05 level.

Table-24.2 shows that the value of t-ratio (= 2.05) is significant at .05 level. It means that arts stream student-teachers of self-financed program (mea = 163.1) have more teaching motivation in comparison to arts stream student-teachers of non-self-financed program.

Table-25.3 : Mean, S.D. and T-ratio Showing the Difference in Teaching Motivation of Student-teachers of Science Stream of Self-financed and Non-self-financed program.

Programme	*N*	*M*	*S.D.*	*t-ratio*
Self-financed	30	167-17	12.7	2.03*
Non-self-financed	20	160.65	10.91	

* Significant at .05 level.

Table-24.3 shows that the value of t-ratio (= 2.03) is significant at .05 level. It means that student-teachers of Science stream of self-financed program have more teaching motivation in comparison to science stream student-teachers of and non-self-financed program.

Thus, it can be concluded that student-teachers of self-financed program have more teaching motivation in comparison to student-teachers of non-self-financed program. This may be due to the reason that student-teachers of self-financed program have paid a handsome amount of money as fees in contrast to the student-teachers of non-self-financed program. Student-teachers of self-financed programme also have higher aspiration to get a job and become a successful teacher. When the teacher remains motivated he develops favorable attitude towards the teaching profession and as a result students not only learn the content taught by the teacher but are also motivated towards learning.

References

1. Kelley, C., Odden, A., Milanowski, A., Heneman, H. (2000). The motivational effects of school-based performance awards. Consortium for Policy Research in Education, University of Pennsylvania.
2. Malmberg, Lars-Eric (2004). Goal-orientation and teacher motivation among teacher applicants and student-teachers. American Educational Research Association 2004. Annual Meeting.
3. Mittal, J.P. (1989). An exploratory study of teachers motivation to work and its relationship with the organizational climate of schools. Ph.D. (Edu.), Meerut University.

4. Upadhyaya, P. (2006). A study of emotional intelligence among student-teachers in relation to academic anxiety, personality traits and teaching motivation. Ph.D. (Edu.) University of Allahabad.

26

Attitude of Student-Teachers: Self-Financed *vs.* Government-Aided Institutions

Mrs Arpita Kumar

In the present scenario, privatization of higher education is viewed as a strategy to reach higher levels of competitive efficiency. The result is the growth of self-financing institutions in large numbers and gaining wide acceptance day by day. It is seen that such institutions are more competitive in providing quality education and mobilising additional resources for public run educational institutions. Such institutions definitely charge higher fee to meet the educational cost but they do not compromise on the standard of education and infrastructure.

In our country, one of the most popular course that is gaining momentum under the self-financing scheme is the B.Ed. course. The success of this course depends upon the attitude of the student-teachers towards teaching. In developing a positive attitude towards teaching, the role of teacher training programme and good infrastructure might play an important part. Hence, the researcher has made an attempt to find out whether the student-teachers pursuing the B.Ed. course in a self-financed institution differ in their attitude towards teaching from the student-teachers pursuing the same course in a government-aided institution.

Objective of the Study

To compare the attitude of student-teachers towards teaching studying in a self-financed and government-aided institution.

Hypothesis

It was hypothesized that "student-teachers studying in a self-financed and government-aided institutions do not differ from one another on their attitude towards teaching."

Methodology

The population of the study consisted of student-teachers of Allahabad city. The sample for this study comprises of 134 student-teachers out of which 50 student-teachers belong to S.S. Khanna Girls' Degree College (self-financed course) and 84 student-teachers belong to K.P. Training College (government aided course). Purposive random sampling technique was employed. For collecting the data, Teacher Attitude Inventory developed by Dr. S.P. Ahluwalia was used. This inventory has 90 likert-type items divided in six sub-scales. Each scale has 15 statements that pertain to a particular aspect of prospective and practicing teacher's professional attitude. The six aspects dealt within the inventory are, attitude towards:

(1) Teaching profession, (2) Classroom teaching, (3) Child centered practices, (4) Educational processes, (5) Pupils, and (6) Teachers.

Table 25.1 shows that the values oft-ratio are significant at .01 level for all the six sub-scales of attitude of student-teachers *viz.* teaching profession, classroom teaching, child-centerd practices, educational process, pupils and teachers. It means that as compared to the student-teachers of government aided institution, student-teachers of self-financed institution have more positive attitude towards teaching profession, classroom teaching, child-centred practices, educational process, pupils and teachers. This may be due to the reason that in the self-financed institution, the fee structure is quite high as compared to the government-aided institution. So, the student-teachers of self-financed institution are provided with better facilities and infrastructure. These students are fortunate enough to get an opportunity to gain practical knowledge in a science, language, social science or a psychology lab besides having access to the use of various audio-visual aids like computers over-head projectors, slides etc. All these things clearly indicate that the institution running self-financed B.Ed. course is more conscientious and aware of the present need and demands of the teaching profession and are striving hard to meet the goals and objectives.

Table-26.1 : Mean, Standard Deviation and T-ratios Showing Differences in Teaching Attitude of Student-teachers

S.N.	*Attitude towards*	*Self-financed Institution* $N_1 = 50$		*Govt.-aided Institution* $N_2 = 84$		*D*	*t*
		M_1	SD_1	M_1	SD_1		
1.	Teaching Profession	43.6	5.695	36.82	6.38	1.0644	6.369*
2.	Classroom Teaching	42.8	5.418	37.416	6.13	1.017	5.294*
3.	Child-centred Practices	46.1	3.455	40.215	6.345	0.8468	6.949*
4.	Educational Process	44.6	5.4	40.035	7.67	1.1415	3.999*
5.	Pupils	42.3	5.51	37.654	6.76	1.0729	4.33*
6.	Teachers	43.0	5.47	36.167	6.85	1.1570	5.90*

*Significant at .01 level.

However, this study is restricted only to one institution running a self-financed B.Ed. course in Allahabad city. It is thereby suggested that this study should further be administered in other self-financing institutions to find out if this result could be generalized. Further, efforts should also be made to restrict the mushroom growth of self-financing institutions having inadequate infrastructure to check the quality control.

References

1. Singh, U.K. and Sudarshan, K.N. (1996), Teacher's Education.
2. Singh, N. (2002), Modernisation of Teacher Education.
3. Stella, A. and Gnanam, A. (2003), Foundation of External Quality Assurance in Indian Higher Education.

27

Privatization of Education *vs.* Commercialization

Dr. Haldhar Yadav

There is no hesitation in admitting that the able state and central governments were findings difficulties in providing adequate funds for the higher and professional education and in opening new professional colleges to meet the growing demands of the increasing number of aspirant, boys and girls. The only alternative available before the government was to allow the entry of private trusts, corporate houses and individual to set-up 'self-financing' institutions to provide education as also qualified manpower.

In the last decade of the century, we have seen the establishment of self-financing college and institution in large number which are providing professional education side by side with the government run colleges and institutions. The purpose of establishing Guru Govind Singh University by the Delhi state government was only to grant affiliation to self-financing colleges, who were interested in running professional course like engineering, medicine, computer science, management, law, education, pharmacy, etc. and good number of college in Delhi were set-up as self-financing colleges.

The self-financing institution in India are doing extremely well and serving the community but there are report also that a good number of self-financing college are only concerned with 'profit earning' and they are least bot hered or concerned towards providing adequate infrastructure competent faculty and suitable academic environment. This is very perturbing as it raises the most pertinent quation concerning the quality of education imparted in the self-financing colleges. This commercial approach of 'Privatization of Education is very dangerous as it amount to exploitation of parent and students.

There are different termmeologies used in the context of liberalization and globalization referred to the Oxford Dictionary IX edition.

Privatization

To provide as district from state control or ownership.

There are at least four types or version of privatization. They are the following :

(i) Extreme version of privatization that implies total privatization, private colleges and universities being managed and funded by the private sector.

(ii) The strong from of the privatization were higher education is publicly provided but cash are fully recovered from the students.

(iii) The moderate form of the privatization were higher education is with a reasonable level of finances mobilized from the non-government sources.

(iv) The pseudo privatization were higher education is privately provided at public expense.

Commercialization means

"Exploit for the purpose of gaining profit."

28

Mushroom Growth of Higher Educational Institution and Quality Control

Vishal Mohan Upadhyay
Pushpendra Gangwar

Introduction

In India financial health of the institutions of higher education has entered a critical phase because India is a developing country and government have limited fund to invest in education. So privatization in education has been vary much prevailing all over the country since long, but the privatization in higher education too did exist, but in a very limited way. There is no hesitation in admitting that the state and central government were finding difficulties in providing adequate funds for the higher and professional education so government, gave green signal to privatization of education and take firm decision to allow entry of private enterprises to set-up self-financing institution. This means the welcome step of the gold to share the burden of over growing demand for admission in to colleges and professional courses.

Different committees and commission from time-to-time have made references to the issue of resources crunch and needed action on the part UGC, MHRD and AICTE, universities and colleges time to time different committee also gave suggestions.

The Gnanam Committee

Stated as Follows: It will not be possible for the State Government to fund adequate resources to create endowments funds for each universities, universities, however should make efforts to rise own resources but must be ensured that there are no conditions attached like preferences in admission etc., raising of resources should not effect academics standards and universities should lay down guideline for the same.

Punnayya Committee

In this report on UGC is as follows: The universities must be strongly encouraged to form partnership with industry it would give universities opportunities to attract additional funds for teaching and research thereby facilitating financial autonomy, access to the latest technology, improved employment prospectus for the student, continuous up-gradation and adaptation of curriculum and improved motivation value in student all this recommendation indicate the relevance, need and significance of improving the financial status of higher education institution by raising resources so that there dependence on government reduced and self-sufficiency is increased.

In 1951, we have 28 universities 695 colleges and 1.7 lakh students and 21,624 teachers. Today there are more then 300 hundred universities, deemed universities and private universities catering to more then 60 lakh students, and with our population is around 110 crore mark. The number of student seeking higher education is likely to touch a figure of 80 lakh.

The system of Indian higher education is one of the largest system in the world and yet inadequate to educate all the youth in the age group of 17–24 yrs. There is rapid growth number of institutions and learners during the past 50 years. There are more then 300 universities and around 11 thousand colleges in the country but neither have they had same status nor same education provide by them. So the question arises on the quality of educations delivering by the institutions. The product of institutions is standing in the rush of unemployed people. They have no knowledge about the subject they have read most of the institutions working as a distributor of degrees and certificated and meaningless. They are meaningless and of no value.

Self-financing and non-aided colleges are quite responsible for the degradation of the level of education. The purpose of running colleges to earn money not to provide education. The management of the college needs more money, so he posses' lots of money burden on students resulting lack of quality in product. So we can say that the last five decade present a picture of light and shade. In the garb of quantitative success there is qualitative failure this is evident from the huge pool of educated persons which indicates massive production of graduate and lack of there employability which in term probably reveals a low standard.

The main reason behind low quality of production in private college of there high fee structure. So the student who are belonging to low economic level are not setting admission. The key point is most of the Indian population, around 60 percent are of poor economical background.

The higher education is on the march with 3 hundred and odd universities and large number of colleges, academic, vocational, technical and management. Our education is a big industry where crores of seasoned and dedicated brand of manpower and the youth are engaged. It requires time to time examination to supply feedback to grow subsequently even by framing new policies and programs.

29

Present Scenario of Educational Research

Dr. M.S. Singh

The beginning of research can be traced back to the pre-historic times when man worked in his search for truth. Search and research have been perenial functions of man to elevate himself in his life. In the primitive man, the nature aroused unlimited curiosity that made him serach for truth about the nature of Nature and about his own status in that Nature. Thus began the philosophical, theological and metaphysical studies. When man began his study of the environmental phenomena to understand that existed around him, and with what he was constantly interacting, there developed physical and natural sciences. When the began to study about the origin of the society and other social phenomana, the social or humanistic sciences originated. His natural endowments, such as intellect, thinking, reasoning, imagination, memory, judgment, ability for analysis and synthesis enabled him to study and experiment with the environment throughout his life-span. Thus, he developed the fund of knowledge which was accumulated and transmitted to posterity as the cultural and social heritage by virtue of his ability for preservation, conservation and communication.

Advanced Leaner's Dictionary of Current English lays

down the meaning of research as "a careful investigation or inquiry specially through search for new facts in any branch of knowledge.

It is doubtful that students can learn much about research design, and research methods without considerable personal involvement of interest, anthusism passonate commitment. Thus I would encourage students to discuss, argue, debate, and even fight about research.

Present Scenario

Researches in India, particularly those engaged in empirical research, are facing several problems. Some of the important problems/present scenario are as follows:

1. The lack of scientific training in the methodology of research is a great impediment for researchers in our country. So that many researchers take a leap in the dark without knowing research methods.
2. Research to many researchers and even to their guides, is mostly a scissor and paste job without any insight shed on the colleted materials. And tendencies to adopt short-cut methods for achieving quick results and to prolong a fellowship unduly for the sake of its immediate material benefits. The consequence is obvious, *viz.,* the research results, quite often, do not reflect the reality or realities.
3. There is insufficient interaction between the university/college research departments, and government departments.
4. Research studies overlapping one another are undertaken quite often for wan of adequate information. This results in duplication and fitters way resources.
5. There does not exist a code of conduct for researcher and inter-university and inter-department rivalries are also quite common.
6. Many researchers in our country also face the difficulty of adequate and timely secretarial assistance, lack of availability of library facilities and lab etc. including computerial assistance. This causes unnecessary delay's in the completion of research studies. And this problem is felt more in libraries

which are away in places from Delhi and/or the state capitals.

7. There is also the difficulty of timely availability of published data from various government and other agencies doing this job in our country.
8. Selection of research problem in education seems to be generally guided by considerations of expediency than of generative value or utility value. M. Phil. and Ph.D. candidates desire to get the degree without much hardword and lapse of time.
9. University/college researches have contributed to quantity rather than quality. Therefore, the standard of research is gradually going down.
10. Researchers often shy away presenting their research proposals or plans, periodic progress statements and draft reports before a group of professionals and other researchers, thereby exposing themselves to searching questions and critical examination of their work.
11. Apart from the UGC and the individual universities with adhoc grants from the UGC, there are few other agencies like ICSSR, NCERT, NCTE offering funds for worthwhile research projects in education. Many are ignorant of such provisions or indifferent to them. Some seem to be discouraged by the formalities. procedures, delays.
12. Support for its research in universities/colleges are not at all adequate. There are programs like COSIST, and SAP which help the universities but the resources available to the UGC are meagre.

Remedies

Through above discussion its needful to give few suggestion for the improvement of present scenario of education research are as follows.

1. A documentation center and a national clearing house in educational research should be developed at the NCERT, UGC and NCTE.
2. Steps should be taken to organise peroidcal conferences of research workers that their isolation

is broken and educational research acquired a professional status simontenously to develop attitude of interdisciplinary research work.

3. It is desirable to set-up a National Academy of Education and Research Council should be set-up in the Ministry of Education. It should consist of representatives of the eminent educationist of universities, training colleges, NCERT and NCTE on the line of National Institute of Science.
4. There is therefore, urgent need to provide good specialized training for research work and services for data-processing, statistical analysis and consultation.
5. It would be the responsibility of the NCERT at the national level and the State Institutes of Education at the state level to bridge the serious gap between educational research and current school practices. A similar role will have to be played by the UGC in the field of higher education.
6. The funding agency should assign or select universities/institutions and team for such purposeful and valuable research. The total expenditure on educational research has to be increased considerably.
7. It is necessary to bring together all the concern officers of the education departments in the filed with the research workers in training colleges and the unviversities and also develop the satisfactory liaison among all concern department.
8. A systematic study of research methodology is an urgent necessity. Before undertaking research projects, researchers should be well-equipped with all the methodological aspects. As such, efforts should be made to provide short duration intensive courses for meeting this requirement.
9. There is the need for generating the confidence that the information/data obtained from a business unit will be misused.
10. There is need for developing a code of conduct not for researchers only but guide also which, if adhered

sincerely, can win over this problem.

11. Efforts should be made for the regular and speedy supply of all governments, private and NGO publications to reach our libraries.
12. Open discussions on their researches should be arranged in departmental research collogues. Departmental and professional growth apart from selecting, planning and promoting useful and sound researches.
13. The limited number of such fellowship need to be awarded to individuals with high grant or funds available could be utilized to provide for research assistants in selected and approved research projects.
14. The professor and head of the department of Education of every university and college should acquire all the information required among the academies.
15. Research is not everbody's cup of tea. But all academics should develop competent research personnel in various fields. The exercises in selecting, designing, planning, conducting and evaluating research must be such as to enhance all the capabilities relating to such tasks and made the persons increasingly competent.

In short, I would like to suggest to Professors/Research Guide, they should morally and strictly follow the code of conduct of research then start and do the research. Every agency of research must collaborate to each others, then we can make a culture and environment of research unless it would be difficult for the country to survive, infact, it would be left behind others.

30

Green Teacher : A Podium for Excellence in Environmental Education

Dr. M.S. Singh

Introduction

Man is a part and parcel of his environment. Due to his interaction with nature on a large scale, the balance of nature have been upset and environmental decadence occurred in most parts of the world. This might be because of environmental pollution or improper and unscientific exploitation of natural resources. It has posed a great problem to the existence of man, plant and animal life on the earth and planet, threatening the quality of man's life and his survival. So, there is a need to increase awareness and understanding of those environments and man's impact upon them and to find out effective ways to manage them. To achieve the above goal, environmental education is the need of the day.

Environmental education is a process to promote the awareness and understanding of the environment, its relationship with man and his activities. It is also aimed at developing responsible actions necessary for preservation, conservation and improvement of the environment and its components. It is the education 'about' the environment 'from' the environment and 'for' the environment. Education about the environment' is acquired an understanding of the total environment. It is learning 'from the environment' when the environment is used as a vehicle for gathering concepts, knowledge and skills related to specific academic disciplines. The development of attitudes, skills and evaluation of abilities for the proper use and the development of the environment is education for the environment.

From Vedic period to modern education. There are only four pillars of 'Learning to know', 'Learning to do 'Learning to live together ' and 'Learning to be all these aspects can be fulfill only through education, education transform in school and society – by the well equipped, competent, skilled, moral, accountable, continuous intellectual researchers/ teachers.

Emerging education horizon in the 21st century world have open up new visitors specially for teacher education in our country. It hardly needs stressing in this frame of reference, new configuration of knowledge in all respect. Present teachers realizing twin obligations towards knowledge and learner. What seems to be more reasonable and promising is draw attention of teacher to certain obligations and commitments and drive from the very nature of the college (NEP 1986).

First of all Centre for Environment Education (CEE) and Commonwealth of Learning (COL) Vancouver, Canada have established the green teacher: Diploma in Environmental Education, a distance education program. The program addresses the rapidly growing need for continuing education and professional development in the field of (EE), and is geared to build capacity of teachers and educators. The Green Teacher offers teachers an opportunity to empower themselves with the requisite knowledge and skills for effective transaction of concepts in environment and development in the classroom. The Green Teacher is open for teachers and other professionals dealing with education and communication for environment and development in a formal teaching learning set-up.

Through above discussion there are main three objectives for Environmental Education to teacher.

- To prepare the teacher to teach environmental education.
- To development awareness about environmental aspects among teachers.
- To prepare the teacher to develop his own curriculum basing on the local requirements.

Suggestions

- The teacher must have a basic understanding of theory, practice and history of field of E.E. This knowledge provides a solid foundation on which teachers can built their won practice.
- Teacher must acknowledge about characters, goal of E.E. and how E.E. is implemented.
- Teachers must understand and accept the responsible associated with practicing E.E. with ongoing learning and professional development.
- A long period of specialized training for teachers and to make unique[definite and essential service.
- A comprehensive self-governing organization of practitioner.
- Greater use of ICT and distance mode both off-line as well as on-line. It can be cast effective and serve large group of teachers.
- E.E. greater correlation curriculum between pre-service and in-service education program for E.E. Curriculum should be update.
- For E.E. on-site program can address related to ground relates of classrooms and teachers work situation and also promotes interaction between teachers and pioneer of environmentalist.
- For E.E. the collaborative participation program should be organized. Established the Forum for exchange of experiences between all this related field pioneers and awareness of newest knowledge about E&EE. Teacher must enable the students to engage in open enquiry and investigation, and teacher should ensure a climate for leaming about exploring the E.
- Teacher must be combine the fundamental of high-

quality education with the unique feature of E.E. to design and implement effective instruction such as– knowledge of learners, knowledge of instructional methodologies, planning for instruction, E.E. materials and resources, recent technology that assist learning, setting for instruction and curriculum planning.

- Teacher must open his eye for observation, enquiry and investigating. E. issues, along with teacher should also intake cooperative learning, community based action research, problem-solving method. Case studies, simulations, models and protect based learning.
- Teacher should acknowledge educational sites, leaming by directly experience oriented learning, express with the senses, developing an ecological aesthetics, behvior and action on leading learning, self-directed leaming in new behvioral norms and exemplary learning.
- Teacher should prepare his/herself for some skill question and analysis, skill of E.L. process and system, skill for understanding and addressing E.L. issues and awareness about the personal and civic responsibility.
- Teacher can independently develop their own teaching learning strategies depending on the demand of each situation. They can also imbibe the concept of environmental education in their routine teaching.

Concluding Remarks

If we follow the above noteworthy discussion such as: Teacher for E. about E from E through his/ her competency, accountability, responsibility and pioneer mentality. Simultaneously teacher has to select a suitable-teaching learning strategy and insert the issues into the brains of the students. In continuation of it the students will try to solve the environmental problems and make he world beautiful. Then he/she will become a green teacher and he/she can transform the school and society.

References

1. Singh Karan(2004), 'Four Pillars of Learning', Anveshika, Indian Journal of Teacher Education, NCTE, New Delhi.
2. Seshadri, C., (2004), 'To Be a Teacher' Anveshika, Indian Journal of Teacher Education, NCTE, New Delhi.
3. Dutta, B.S., (1998), *Environmental Education:* 'The Need of the Hour.'
4. *Environmental Educational, Problem & Prospects.* Discovery Publication House, New Delhi.
5. Rao & Prasad (1998), Environmental Education. 'The Need of the Hour.'
6. *Environmental Educational, Problem & Prospects.* Teaching, Learning, Strategies in Environmental Education. Discovery Publication House, New Delhi.
7. Dass, Swain (1998), 'E.E. at the School Level' *Environmental Educational, Problem & Prospects.* Discovery Publication House, New Delhi.
8. Rao, V.K. & Reddy, R.S. (1997), 'Environmental Education.' Commonwealth Publication, New Delhi. Green Teacher (2006) 'Centre for E.E. Lko. (CEE) Commonwealth Learning.

31

Self-Financing of Higher Education: Issues and Challenges

Dr. M.S. Singh

The privatization of Higher Education (HE) is not a new phenomenon in India and elsewhere. After the Second World War (1945) and in the Indian context of post-independence (1947), the world has seen an enormous expansion of Higher Education. Traditionally under-represented groups gained access to HE and the student numbers expanded rapidly. However, state finances have largely remained stable after the 1970s. This has led to the entry of 'for-profit' entrepreneurs in the market of higher education. The politicians, administrators, business and to some extent the academia have joined hands in loosening the control of the state structure of HE. 'For-profit' private institutions developed, where Higher Education is, in many cases, affordable to the lucky few, who can afford to pay. Public systems have in many cases been cut back to the benefit of for-profit education of offered by private institutions.

The recent phenomenon of self-financing educational institutions, have been facilitated by the several factors like, low access rate *i.e.*7 percent. Indian system of higher education, in spite of being one the largest system of higher education of the world, uneven quality of education, rigidity of conventional university system and its unwillingness to innovate and change, intense need for education commensurate to world class standards due to globalization and shift in government's priority for education resulting in curtailed outlay for higher education.

Issues

The present paper consist between two big issues such as "Trading of Education" and "Role of Education". The protagonists of both the schools of thought have strong arguments. Without having the clear understanding of both the perspectives, it is not possible to develop any rational policy framework. Let us first analyse both the arguments.

Trading of Education

The first and the foremost issue that has become a matter of hot debate and concern amongst all affected groups is 'trading of education'. The argument of protagonists of privatization is "The supply of education should be according to the individual and market needs. There should be free access of market players. The education is being treated as a 'product and the students as 'consumers'. There should be free completion in the market place. The market players should be able to select a product enter the market 'for-profit'. If the product is not in demand, they should be able to drop it or exit the market."

First, market mechanisms will stimulate competition between Higher Education Institutions and that this will inevitably lead to a higher degree of quality, better adjustment of supply to demand and more efficiency in the provision of Higher Education.

Second, the tuition fees represent a contribution of the student to the study costs and will lead to a more quickly finishing of studies as well as creating a consumer mentality among students.

The Role of Education

"Education serves several purposes in societies, the most important ones being its role as a means for social development and democratic empowerment and advancing of the general well-being and economic competitiveness of societies, means of accumulating and sharing knowledge and cultural capital as well as a means for personal growth and well-being. Because of these multiple role in constructing of societies, the question is should education be reduced to a mere economic, tradable commodity?"

The concept of the 'student as a consumer' and education as a product' fails to acknowledge the importance of education as a social tool and runs counter to the creation of knowledge based society with democratic, tolerant and active citizens.

The concept of education as mere tradable product jeopardises the academic freedom of universities, as markets fail and a sell-out of education might lead to decreasing diversity and freedom of research in institutions of Higher Education.

International systems can be transplanted but the moot question remains can the countries like India harness the benefits for the society at large given the environment prevailing in such countries. The argument is an elitist group is created that States its own society and country and waits for the opportunity to migrate. The counter argument is purely economic. Let us export intellectual property; convert it into money and repatriate it back to the country of origin. The offer of dual citizenship to NRIs is the result of such a psyche.

The new daunting task before Department of Teacher Education, which are given a new norm (M.A. B.Ed.) by NCTE, New Delhi, Teacher should be appointed as B.Ed. Lecturer. It is biggest challenge before the Teacher Educated to sustain the quality of Teacher Education. The state agencies, society and academia would be to sustain the quality, national needs, affordable fee structures and stop the co-modification of education.

A Way Out

Any policy framework on higher education must take into account the conflicting and contradictory positions that prevail in India and achieve a balance in them. Some of the aspects that need to be considered are:

- The quality of Teacher Education may be sustain through previous norm of the teacher appointment.

- Higher Education needs to be liberalized and the shackles of "Licence Permit Raj" need to be removed.
- Multiplicity of agencies needs to be reduced.
- Private sector (both Indian and foreign) investment in higher education should be encouraged. It should not be restrictive.
- The role State Governments, AICTE, NCTE, Universities and UGC need to be seen afresh.
- The affiliation by the universities outside their jurisdiction within India is matter of grave concern and debate as it is presently governed by commercial considerations. The key factor is that many affiliating universities do not have resources to monitor the functioning of such institutions.
- AICTE, UGC and NCTE acts should clearly spell out the role of State Governments in India vis-a-vis technical institutes and universities especially for private self-financing institutes. NOC from the State Governments must be perpetual and not the annual ritual that breeds interference and corruption in management of higher education.
- Once a State Government issues NOC, the affiliating University should supervise the quality of education and implementation of other norms laid down by AICTE, UGC and NCTE as the case may be. The affiliating universities must create necessary infrastructure for monitoring.
- AICTE, UGC and NCTE should inspect the self-financing institutes not more than once in three years. More than this frequency is self-defeating that adds to the cost of education and has overtones of interference. Besides this AICTE and the affiliating university should jointly inspect an affiliated institution. The role of State Governments, in this respect, has already been discussed above.
- The fee structure is another problem area especially for self-financing institutions. There has been protracted litigation on this subject. Hon. Supreme Court's judgment on this subject is well intentioned and in the right spirit.

Beside the above discussion points there are so many points such as infrastructure facilities, faculty shortage and satisfaction, high salary expectations and job hopping also big issues are also prevailing in the problem of self-financing higher education. Therefore its needful to see the all issues in global form with the collaboration of UGC, NCTE, Central and State Government can salve the self-financing higher education problem. If you want to survive and maintained the quality of teacher education we must start joint effort to remove the new norm of the Teacher Education.

References

1. Dick, M and Carey, L. (1996). *The Systematic Design of Instruction (4th Ed.)* Harper Collins.
2. Lockwood, Fred (1992). Alternative methods of materials production. *Media and Technology for Human Resource Development 4(4)* 233-238.
3. The Open University (1997), *Guide of Quality Assurance in the Open University,* Milton Keynes. November 19-20.
4. Chaturvedi, S., *Privatisation of Higher Education: Issues and Challenges,* University News, Vol. 43.

32

Quality Concern about Teaching Process: Teacher Education

Dr. M.S. Singh

"Education is the cradle of success, it is the vital key of nations." Administrators, educationists and policy makers across the country are recognizing that education system needs fundamental changes to keep pace with an increasingly complex global society. Education should not only reflect the needs of the society but should also emphasize excellence. Every effort should be made to adopt our educational system according to todays changing economical and social realities.

In our increasingly complex and rapidly changing society, teacher's tasks are more demanding and changing than ever before. The teacher play a vital and significant role in educating the future generations and in contributing to national and international development and prosperity. Teacher Education and appropriate pedagogy is thus very important as it enables them to discharge their responsibility successfully.

Quality in all walks of life is discussed today by every nation. Everyone admits that quality of education is the base for the quality of human life. Every nation, therefore, strives for improvement in the quality of education and gives emphasis on the quality of teacher education to realize the desired end of education. The teacher education program, thus, comes in the forefront. Teacher education will always have to solicit answers to four basic-questions and offer opportunities to realize them in a great variety of educational situations, that is : What are the objectives of education? How do the objectives vary from individual to individual? How can the objectives be achieved? and how does one know that they have been achieved?

For quality education, the objectives of teacher education may be classified under three categories:

- Cognitive (knowledge and understanding);
- Psychomotor (skills); and
- Affective (attitudes, appreciation, values etc.)

The quality of teacher education will, prima facie, depend on the quality of students admitted to the teacher education course. Since these teachers may be required to teach up to Class VIII, admission is made strictly on the basis of merit, subject to reservation of seats as per the state policy. It is also desirable that candidates are selected on the basis of state level selection test, focusing on teacher and teaching aptitude.

Quality

Webster's dictionary describes the word 'quality' as a degree of excellence and superiority in kind. Quality is a concept which is also considered essential for industry. Now-a-days education and industry have moved closer borrowing ideas and practices from each other. Hence most of the educationist adopted the meaning of quality as the ability to meet the stated purpose for which the service was offered. Dina Green (1994) points out. Quality may be associated with; *(i)* The providing of a product or service that is distinctive or special, *(ii)* the conformation to a specification or standard, *(iii)* the effectiveness in meeting instructional goals or *(iv)* the Meeting of customer's need.

Quality in Teacher Education

Quality in teacher education means not only the inculcation of knowledge, quality, and competencies but also it means creating the appropriate atmosphere for the development of a teacher. It includes the acquirement of new efficient trends, techniques, methods. In TEP, we should also create awareness towards national goals, values and demands of the society. For this we must think about the following:

(i) Quality syllabus: Quality syllabus which includes upgrading and updating of syllabus, credibility of the content, sensitivity towards the self and social development.

(ii) Quality faculty: Academic and research qualification, intellectual ability to built knowledge, communicating skills.

(iii) Quality teaching, training and evaluation: Quality teaching, training and evaluation means interactive and participatory character. Innovating methods of teaching and training, regularity, students enthusiasm towards attending the classes, teacher-trainee relationship and modes and tools of evaluation.

(iv) Quality research: Quality research means usability of research, generating paradigm shifts, research publication and quality of character. It means the attitude of the teacher towards his role in the changing world and his dedication towards the social change.

The need for quality teachers has always been emphasised for preparing future citizens for facing the changing society. The quality competence and character of teachers are significant factors for influencing the society. Teacher Education Programmes (TEP) aim at supplying teachers to our educational institutions. Hence such TEPs play a vital role in our national development.

Evidence

Research studies, focused on the characteristics of educational development in the country, suggest that there has been a 'positive spurt' in quantity and a 'negative spurt' in the quality of overall education. Research carried out with respect to primary and secondary education stages usually concludes that teacher-education is the prime subject. It is argued that teacher training seems to have no bearing on what the prospective teachers do in the classroom, when they join their teaching position after completing the training ritual.

An assessment on the efficacy of teacher education programme revealed:

- Inadequate demonstration.of the basic teaching skills in the actual classroom situation.
- Mismatch between the optimal teaching competency and the exhibited teaching competency in the actual classroom situation.
- Incongruence between teaching aptitude and teaching performance.
- Scanty exposure on practice teaching.

Adequate need for essentials on teacher efficiency, viz.

(i) Learner-centered management;
(ii) Planning instructional management;
(iii) Subject-based management;and
(iv) Communication efficiency.

Portfolios

Portfolios are collections of purposeful and specialized work, capturing a process that can never be fully appreciated unless one can be inside and outside someone else's mind. They validate current expectations and legitimize the future goals. They tell us what to see and what we wish we would not see. They are a professional looking glass. Portfolios can be developed in each and every context in the curriculum transaction.

Teachers are the key persons in curriculum transaction. They are to perceive every component in the teaching-learning process through portfolios. A teacher education portfolio is designed on eight steps through which the objectives are meticulously spelt out for ensuring quality in teacher education. The eight-fold interactive steps in the teacher education portfolio are:

1. Developing appropriate observation strategies for teacher demonstration,
2. Designing and implementing adequate training on classroom interaction analysis,
3. Orienting teachers towards matching learning-styles and teaching-styles,
4. Sensitizing the teacher towards psycho-technological principles in the preparation of teaching-learning material.
5. Ensuring competency-based teaching.

6. Observation of video clippings on various teaching methodologies.
7. Reflections on practice teaching.
8. Incorporation of reflection and inquiry.

The whole system of teacher education functions on the basis of observation and interaction between the teacher educator and the teacher trainees. The teacher educator observes the teaching efficiency of the student teacher. The observations have to be done systematically. A checklist can be developed, incorporating factors for teacher efficiency such as general disposition, subject-based management and support strategies. After an observation, a discussion should follow for explicit assessment.

It so happens that individuals of differing performance levels as student teachers do not differ in their transfer skills in the school campus. The fact that the teacher is an expert in a subject is a no guarantee that the teacher can help others learn the subject. They need thorough orientation on teaching-strategies and learning-styles during internship.

Suggestions

- It is needles to mention that the teachers should achieve full mastery over the content competencies. Moreover the responsibility of training college will not end by giving the pupil teacher some nodding acquaintance of the tricks of the trade, but it has to develop in him a growing understanding of human growth and development and of the process of learning.
- Regarding, the realization of the contexture competencies and conceptual competencies the teacher should have a thorough idea about social problem and the impact of socio-economic and socio-cultural factors on the children to be taught.
- In our B.Ed. curriculum, we can hardly see any scope to go to the society and study the socio-economic problems of the neighboring society. So it is necessary for the secondary teachers training program to be based on socio-economic and cultural needs of the society.

- Special emphasis to be given on the transactional competencies.
- Teaching-learning process in education involves interaction between the teacher and the taught resulting in the achievement of the desired competencies. So it is the responsibility of teacher training colleges to develop all the competencies in student teachers.
- The teachers of today are regarded not only as disseminators of knowledge but also as motivators, the mediators and the facilitators of learning so it is necessary for student-teachers that proper orientation and training should be provided to them and for that new dimensions must be added to teacher education program. It is the responsibility of the teacher training colleges to prepare student teachers to meet emerging needs and challenges of modern times. In this direction, the appropriate utilization of information communication technology can be used effectvely.
- The research findings indicate the need to identify the gaps and explore changes required in the existing education program that will respond to the actual needs of the natural classrooms. The system of teacher education cannot be judged independently to see its value and consequences. It needs substantive documents, that is, the portfolios collected, now and then. as evidence to see the system in its totality.

References

1. Havinghurst Robert, J., *Development at Tasks and Education.* Longmans green and Company London, 1949.
2. National Council for Teacher Education (1998) Assessment and Evaluation in Teacher Education, NOTE. Monograph Series 98/6, New Delhi.
3. National Council for Teacher Education (1998), Quality Concerns in Secondary Teacher Education, NCTE Monograph Series, 98/26, New Delhi.

4. Thakare, Anjali P., *Director of Physical Education,* Shri. Shivaji College of Education, Amravati.
5. Singh, Om Prakash, Singh, Ramakant, *"Quality Improvement in Teacher Education", Seminar* on Quality Impact on Education.

33

Qualitative Paradigm Shifting from Conventional System to Modern Approach in Distance Education

Dr. M.S. Singh

The proliferation of information and communication technology during the past three decades and its demonstrated application for successful teaching and learning at a distance has led to a paradigm shift in the teaching and learning at the higher education level. This article analyzes this fundamental paradigm shift and reflects upon its implications for modern approach in distance education.

In reflecting over the concept of distance education, it is necessary to distinguish between the two senses in which the term education is used. Education first refers to the learning process—that is the mental process of intermeshing an external event in order to understand in and control it. Second education could also refer to the infrastructure which makes possible the learning processes—school and college buildings, material and equipment, laboratories, playground etc. The teacher and the book and increasingly today the various forms of audio-visual aids occupy a middle position between the learning process and its infrastructure. The teacher, the book, the electronic aids are, part of the learning process in the sense that they help in the internalsing process:

in fact the teacher is in many cases a part and hierarchically above the book and the audio-visual aid, because he has to interpret the content of the book and explain the message that the electronic instrument conveys. On the other hand, the teacher in a part from the learner and has to be paid a salary and assured living conditions, the book has to be purchased, at is the audio-visual aid, and in that sense all three are part of the infrastructure.

Essential to the understanding of the educational paradigm shifts under consideration, it may be useful to analyze the shifts in educational thinking as a consequence of the emergence of the technology in a historical perspective. Historically teaching and learning underwent quite a number of changes, drastic ones over. For example, long back the introduction of the technology of writing replaced the oral tradition of teaching and learning to a great extent. 1800 years later print and the availability of books changed instruction drastically, as more people could learn than could be present in the face-to-face situation. Especially, the nature and the meaning of the academic lecture was altered—to mention one aspect of this change. The nineteenth century saw the advent of the railways and postal services—this led to the development of correspondence education. And in our century the protagonists of the audio-visual media, radio and television changed our notion of teaching and learning significantly and we saw the popularization of distance education.

Challenges and Problems Facing ICT

The fear of technology*

- Lack of financial proficiency in using e-learning.
- Lack of awareness of opportunities offered by ICT-based teaching/learning to allow adequate exploitation.
- Lack of a comprehensive and high quality collection of online information resources to support teaching learning and research.
- Restricted access to the main information.
- Lack of human touch, affective domain, diagnostic and remedial learning and us psychological system.

Although these changes were significant and full of consequences but none of them and not even all put together can compare with the drastic changes in education and the consequences which are caused by the educational paradigm shifts which we are witnessing today due to the progress made in the network technology and the digitalization of communication and information technology. Never before in the history of education was there any educational reform tackled in so many countries all over the world simultaneously. The educational paradigm shifts are a global phenomenon and a global issue today. The 18th ICDE world conference at the Penn State University was an ample proof of this Today Negroponte's slogan 'Distance is dead' and McLuhan's prediction of 'Global Village' have become relalities.

Looking closer at the phenomenon, it is revealed that a great number of very specific paradigm shifts have already taken place which have driven us into the situation we are in today. And many shifts are clearly foreseeable as we become capable if integrating the digital network communication technologies in our existing systems of traditional and distance systems of education. These shifts can be identified in the cultural, social, political, and economic conditions of education. In the coming sections, I have made a humble attempt to highlight the paradigm shifts in higher education that have already taken place and those which are fore–seeable in the near future.

Modern Approach

The successful spread of distance education, incorporating the multi-media technologies, has already resulted in the following paradigm shifts which have drastically changed our traditional notions about education in general and higher education in particular:

- There has been a definite shift the education of children and juveniles to the education of adults. The much propagated concept of lifelong learning is the result of this shift, which gave rise to continuing education and university tuition for adults through distance education.

- Best exemplified by the emergence of open universities and the trend is towards the democratization of highly education if not mass higher education. More and more an elitist paradigm is substituted by an egalitarian one.
- A significant shift has been there in our concept of students. Till recently they were mostly males, juveniles who lived and studied on the campuses of the colleges or universities. Today notions are changed. Now, a substantial number of them are female, many are older or even much older.
- Today, as an impact of distance education, a shift of emphasis with regard to the goals of higher education is clearly visible. Whereas the traditional universities offered a more general and all round education, the multi-media universities are offering more and more specific and specialized courses. Today the autonomous and self-sufficient universities are showing an increased willingness of co-operating with the industries. Public private projects are at a premium.
- In essence there has been a shift from monastic seclusion and academic exclusiveness with regard to research and teaching to open competition with other providers of education.
- As we become capable of entering the eradigital communication dramatic paradigm shifts will also occur in the digitalized learning environment.
- Imagine if the students have an access to all information in the world, to all teaching programs, to electronic books, to electronic libraries and to all the intelligent expert systems.
- To learn what they want to learn, the students will have to develop their abilities to self-instruction and of becoming autonomous learners. They have to exhibit new skills in performing activities unknown the them.
- These programs are to help the students in their endeavor to become independent and self-regulated learners. This means the culture of expository

reaching is being substituted by the culture of autonomous learning.

- **Security:** The creation and maintenance of a secure teaching and learning environment and the internet with authenticated access to require resources, enabling confidential transactions to be carried out conveniently and safely.
- A comprehensive set to advisory and Consultancy Services to help institutions explore and ploit the internet safely, legally and effectively along with other IT applications for learning, teaching, research and e-business.
- **Collaboration:** The need for encouraging an appreciation of the global nature of ICT and associated applications to foster collaboration for effective international competition.

Finally, the existing traditional universities will also face the music of these paradigm shift in distance education. If they are to serve their role as agents of change, they have to become flexible and open up according to the expectations of the times and the marked demands. They will have option but adapt, the distance education methods may come to their rescue. If we analyze the existing scenario we find they are no longer responsible for planning well-developed oral presentations and organizing and conducting classes. They are no longer the experts in conveying knowledge. Rather they will have to assume new functions as tutors, counselors and facilitators. And if they are ambitious they may take up assignments of developing and designing hypertexts and hypermedia programs in their specialized fields of knowledge.

Index

●●●